DISINTE-
GRATION

Also by Eugene Robinson

Coal to Cream
Last Dance in Havana

DISINTE-GRATION

| The Splintering of
Black America |

EUGENE ROBINSON

Doubleday
New York   London   Toronto
Sydney   Auckland

DD

DOUBLEDAY

All rights reserved. Published in the United States by Doubleday,
a division of Random House, Inc., New York, and in Canada by
Random House of Canada Limited, Toronto.

www.doubleday.com

DOUBLEDAY and the DD colophon are registered
trademarks of Random House, Inc.

Book design by Michael Collica

Library of Congress Cataloging-in-Publication Data
Robinson, Eugene, 1954–
Disintegration : the splintering of Black America / Eugene
Robinson.—1st ed.
p. cm.
Includes bibliographical references.
1. African Americans—Social conditions—21st century. 2. African
Americans—Economic conditions—21st century. 3. African
Americans—Race identity. 4. Group identity—United States.
5. Social classes —United States. 6. Social mobility—United States.
7. United States—Social conditions—21st century. 8. United
States—Race relations. I. Title.
E185.86.R618 2010
305.896'073—dc22   2010020405

ISBN 978-0-385-52654-8

PRINTED IN THE UNITED STATES OF AMERICA

1 3 5 7 9 10 8 6 4 2

First Edition

To Mrs. Louisa S. Robinson
from her loving son

CONTENTS

ACKNOWLEDGMENTS

Disintegration could not have been written without the incisive, timely, good-natured, and sometimes positively uncanny contributions of Kris Puopolo, my editor at Doubleday, who often knew precisely what I was trying to say before I did. I also owe a tremendous debt to my literary agent, Rafe Sagalyn, who believed in this project from the beginning and was utterly committed to making it a reality.

A book-in-progress is like a new member of the author's household—a fussy, demanding weekend guest who never left—and my wonderful wife, Avis Collins Robinson, welcomed this interloper with unfailing patience and grace; she even came up with the title, among many other substantive contributions.

My editors at *The Washington Post,* Fred Hiatt and Autumn Brewington, and at the Washington Post Writers Group, Alan Shearer and Jim Hill, gave me the time and space I needed to write the book; I am in their debt. And I owe special thanks to the many distinguished scholars whose research I cite in these pages. Any errors of analysis or interpretation are mine, not theirs.

DISINTE-
GRATION

1

"BLACK AMERICA" DOESN'T LIVE HERE ANYMORE

I t was one of those only-in-Washington affairs, a glittering A-list dinner in a stately mansion near Embassy Row. The hosts were one of the capital's leading power couples—the husband a wealthy attorney who famously served as consigliere and golfing partner to presidents, the wife a social doyenne who sat on all the right committees and boards. The guest list included enough bold-faced names to fill the *Washington Post*'s Reliable Source gossip column for a solid week. Most of the furniture had been cleared away to let people circulate, but the elegant rooms were so thick with status, ego, and ambition that it was hard to move.

Officially the dinner was to honor an aging lion of American business: the retired chief executive of the world's biggest media and entertainment company. Owing to recent events, however, the distinguished mogul was eclipsed at his own party. An elegant businesswoman from Chicago—a stranger to most of the other guests—suddenly had become one of the capital's most important power brokers, and this exclusive soiree was serving as her unofficial debut in Washington society. The bold-faced names feigned nonchalance but were desperate to meet her. Eyes followed the woman's every move; ears strained to catch her every word. She pretended not to mind being stalked from room to room by eager supplicants and would-be best friends. As the evening went on, it became apparent that while the other guests were taking her measure, she was systematically taking theirs. To every beaming, glad-handing, air-kissing approach she responded with the Mona Lisa smile of a woman not to be taken lightly.

Others there that night included a well-connected lawyer who would soon be nominated to fill a key cabinet post; the chief executive of one of the nation's leading cable-television networks; the former chief executive of the mortgage industry's biggest firm; a gaggle of high-powered lawyers; a pride of investment bankers; a flight of social butterflies; and a chattering of well-known cable-television pundits, slightly hoarse and completely exhausted after spending a full year in more or less continuous yakety-yak about the presidential race. By any measure, it was a top-shelf crowd.

On any given night, of course, some gathering of the great and the good in Washington ranks above all others by virtue of exclusivity, glamour, or the number of Secret Service SUVs parked outside. What makes this one worth noting is that all the luminaries I have described are black.

The affair was held at the home of Vernon Jordan, the smooth, handsome, charismatic confidant of Democratic presidents, and his wife, Ann, an emeritus trustee of the John F. Kennedy Center for the Performing Arts and a reliable presence at every significant social event in town. Known for his impeccable political instincts, Jordan had made the rare mistake of backing the wrong candidate in the 2008 primaries—his friend

Hillary Clinton. There are no grudges in Vernon's world, however; barely a week after the election, he was already skillfully renewing his ties with the Obama crowd.

The nominal guest of honor was Richard Parsons, the former CEO of Time Warner Inc. Months earlier, he had relinquished his corner office on Columbus Circle to tend the Tuscan vineyard that friends said was the favorite of his residences.

The woman who stole the show was Valerie Jarrett, one of Obama's best friends and most trusted advisers. A powerful figure in the Chicago business community, Jarrett was unknown in Washington until Obama made his out-of-nowhere run to capture the Democratic nomination and then the presidency. Suddenly she was the most talked-about and sought-after woman in town. Everyone understood that she would be sitting on the mother lode of the capital's rarest and most precious asset: access to the president of the United States.

Others sidling up to the buffet included Eric Holder, soon to be nominated as the nation's first black attorney general, and his wife, Sharon Malone, a prominent obstetrician; Debra Lee, the longtime chief of Black Entertainment Television and one of the most powerful women in the entertainment industry; Franklin Raines, the former CEO of Fannie Mae, a central and controversial figure in the financial crisis that had begun to roil markets around the globe; and cable-news regulars Donna Brazile and Soledad O'Brien from CNN, Juan Williams from Fox News Channel, and, well, me from MSNBC—all of us having talked so much during the long campaign that we were sick of hearing our own voices.

The glittering scene wasn't at all what most people have in mind when they talk about black America—which is one reason why so much of what people say about black America makes so little sense. The fact is that asking what something called "black America" thinks, feels, or wants makes as much sense as commissioning a new Gallup poll of the Ottoman Empire. Black America, as we knew it, is history.

* * *

There was a time when there were agreed-upon "black leaders," when there was a clear "black agenda," when we could talk confidently about "the state of black America"—but not anymore. Not after decades of desegregation, affirmative action, and urban decay; not after globalization decimated the working class and trickle-down economics sorted the nation into winners and losers; not after the biggest wave of black immigration from Africa and the Caribbean since slavery; not after most people ceased to notice—much less care—when a black man and a white woman walked down the street hand in hand. These are among the forces and trends that have had the unintended consequence of tearing black America to pieces.

Ever wonder why black elected officials spend so much time talking about purely symbolic "issues," like an official apology for slavery? Or why they never miss the chance to denounce a racist outburst from a rehab-bound celebrity? It's because symbolism, history, and old-fashioned racism are about the only things they can be sure their African American constituents still have in common.

Barack Obama's stunning election as the first African American president seemed to come out of nowhere, but it was the result of a transformation that has been unfolding for decades. With implications both hopeful and dispiriting, black America has undergone a process of disintegration.

Disintegration isn't something black America likes to talk about. But it's right there, documented in census data, economic reports, housing patterns, and a wealth of other evidence just begging for honest analysis. And it's right there in our daily lives, if we allow ourselves to notice. Instead of one black America, now there are four:

- a Mainstream middle-class majority with a full ownership stake in American society
- a large, Abandoned minority with less hope of escaping poverty and dysfunction than at any time since Reconstruction's crushing end
- a small Transcendent elite with such enormous wealth, power, and influence that even white folks have to genuflect
- two newly Emergent groups—individuals of mixed-race heritage and communities of recent black immigrants—that make us wonder what "black" is even supposed to mean

These four black Americas are increasingly distinct, separated by demography, geography, and psychology. They have different profiles, different mind-sets, different hopes, fears, and dreams. There are times and places where we all still come back together—on the increasingly rare occasions when we feel lumped together, defined, and threatened solely on the basis of skin color, usually involving some high-profile instance of bald-faced discrimination or injustice; and in venues like "urban" or black-oriented radio, which serves as a kind of speed-of-light grapevine. More and more, however, we lead separate lives.

And where these distinct "nations" rub against one another, there are sparks. The Mainstream tend to doubt the authenticity of the Emergent, but they're usually too polite, or too politically correct, to say so out loud. The Abandoned accuse the Emergent—the immigrant segment, at least—of moving into Abandoned neighborhoods and using the locals as mere stepping-stones. The immigrant Emergent, with their intact families and long-range mind-set, ridicule the Abandoned for being their own worst enemies. The Mainstream bemoan the plight of the Abandoned—but express their deep concern from a distance. The Transcendent, to steal the old line about Boston society, speak only to God; they are idolized by the Mainstream and the Emergent for the obstacles they have overcome, and by the Abandoned for the shiny things they own. Mainstream, Emergent, and Transcendent all lock their car doors when they drive through an Abandoned neighborhood. They think the Abandoned don't hear the disrespectful *thunk* of the locks; they're wrong.

How did this breakup happen? It's overly simplistic to draw a straight line from "We Shall Overcome" to "Get Rich or Die Tryin'," but that's the general trajectory.

Forty years ago, after major cities from coast to coast had gone up in flames, black equaled poor. Roughly six in ten black Americans were barely a step ahead of the bill collector, with fully 40 percent of the total living in the abject penury that the Census Bureau officially labels "poverty" and another 20 percent earning a bit more but still basically poor. Over the next three decades—as civil rights laws banned discrimination in education, housing, and employment, and as affirmative action offered life-changing opportunities to those prepared to take advantage—millions of black households clawed their way into the Mainstream and the black poverty rate fell steadily, year after year. By the mid-'90s, it was down to 25 percent—and then the needle got stuck. Today, roughly one-quarter of black Americans—the Abandoned—remain in poverty.[1]

And the poorest of these poor folks are actually losing ground. In 2000, 14.9 percent of black households reported income of less than $10,000 (in today's dollars); in 2005, the figure was 17.1 percent.[2] Demographically, the Abandoned constitute the youngest black America; they are also by far the least suburban, living for the most part in core urban neighborhoods and the rural South.

Those who made it into the Mainstream, however, have continued their rise. In 1967, only one black household in ten made $50,000 a year; now three of every ten black families earn at least that much. More strikingly, four decades ago not even *two black households in a hundred* earned the equivalent of more than $100,000 a year. Now almost one black household in ten has crossed that threshold to the upper middle class—joining George and Louise Jefferson in that "dee-luxe apartment in the sky," perhaps, or living down the street from the Huxtables' handsomely appointed brownstone. All told, the four black Americas control an estimated $800 billion in purchasing power—roughly the GDP of the thirteenth-richest nation on earth. Most of that money is made and spent by the Mainstream.[3]

Here's another way to look at it: Forty years ago, if you found yourself among a representative all-black crowd, you could assume that nearly half the people around you were poor, poorly educated, and underemployed. Today, if you found yourself at a representative gathering of black adults, four out of five would be solidly middle class.

And some African Americans have soared far higher. A friend of mine who lives in Chicago once took a flight on the Tribune Company's corporate jet. Noticing a much larger, newer, fancier private jet parked on the tarmac nearby, he asked his boss whose it was. The answer: "Oprah's." The all-powerful Winfrey is one of the African Americans who have soared highest of all, into the realm of the Transcendent. There have long been black millionaires—Madam C. J. Walker, who built an empire on hair-care products in the early twentieth century, is often cited as the first. But never before have African Americans presided as full-fledged Masters of the Universe over some of the biggest firms on Wall Street (Richard Parsons, Kenneth Chenault, Stanley O'Neal). There have been wealthy black athletes since Jack Johnson, but never before have they transformed themselves into such savvy tycoons (Michael Jordan, Tiger Woods). And while African Americans have made billions for the music industry over the years, even pioneers such as Berry Gordy Jr. and Quincy Jones never owned and controlled as big a chunk of the business as today's hip-hop moguls (Russell Simmons, P. Diddy, Jay-Z).

And the Emergent? They're the product of two separate phenomena. First, there has been a flood of black immigrants from Africa and the Caribbean. In 1980, the census reported 816,000 foreign-born black people in the United States; by the 2000 census, that figure had more than tripled to 2,815,000.[4] You might question my use of the word "flood" for numbers that seem relatively small in absolute terms, but consider these newcomers' outsize impact: Half or more of the black students entering elite universities such as Harvard, Princeton, and Duke these days are the sons and daughters of African immigrants.[5] This makes sense when you consider that their parents are the best-educated immigrant group in America, with more advanced degrees than the Asians, the Europeans, you name it. (They're far better educated than native-born Americans, black or white.) But their children's educational success leads Mainstream and Abandoned black Americans to ask whether affirmative action and other programs designed to foster diversity are reaching the people they were intended to help—the systematically disadvantaged descendants of slaves.

The second Emergent phenomenon is the acceptance of interracial marriage, once a crime and until recently a novelty. A University of Michigan study found that in 1990, nearly one married black man in ten was wed to a white woman—and roughly one married black woman in twenty-five was wed to a white man. These figures, the researchers found, had increased eightfold over the previous four decades.[6] Barack Obama, the man who would be president; Adrian Fenty, the mayor of Washington, D.C.; Jordin Sparks, a winner on *American Idol*—all are the product of black-white marriages. And the boomer-echo generation, raised on a diet of diversity, has even fewer hang-ups about race and relationships.

In a sense, though, we're just headed back to the future. Harvard scholar Henry Louis Gates Jr. recently produced a public-television series in which he used genealogical research and DNA testing to unearth the heritage of several prominent African Americans. When he sent his own blood off to be tested, Gates discovered to his surprise that more than 50 percent of his genetic material was European. Wider DNA testing has shown that nearly one-third of all African Americans trace their heritage to a white male ancestor—likely a slave owner.

So forget about whether the mixed-race Emergents are "black enough." How black am I? How black can any of us claim to be?

* * *

This gradual but relentless fragmentation—economic, geographic, psychological, cultural—is by now undeniable. In 2007, a remarkable study by the Pew Research Center came up with a finding that made my jaw drop: An incredible 37 percent of African Americans agreed with the statement that "blacks today can no longer be thought of as a single race because the black community is so diverse."[7]

To someone like me who grew up in the Jim Crow era of separate but unequal, this is profoundly unsettling. I left the South at sixteen to go to college and, like many of my peers, went through a process of interrogating my identity. But that phase ran its course long ago, and I knew without the slightest doubt who I was: a black man in America. Now is there some question about what being "a black man in America" even means? Has a true-false exam suddenly become multiple-choice?

The Pew study found that black Americans whose incomes placed them in the vast, struggling middle—earning between $30,000 and $100,000 a year—were the most likely to believe that black people no longer constituted one race. Black Americans at the top of the scale, with incomes of more than $100,000 a year, were most likely to cling to the more traditional view that "blacks can still be thought of as a single race because they have so much in common." Perhaps we should begin to think of racial solidarity as a luxury item.

As a thought experiment, wind the clock back precisely forty years and try to imagine how different that evening at the Jordans' would have been.

In 1968, it was possible to defend the generalization that black equaled poor—and easy to defend the statement that black certainly did not equal rich. With only 2 percent of black households earning the equivalent of $100,000 a year or more, there simply wouldn't have been many African American families that could afford to host such a lavish social event, complete with liveried waiters and a well-stocked open bar.

Even in 1968, though, Washington was a magnet for the upwardly mobile black middle class and the tiny black upper crust. The city has been home to a significant black elite since before the days of Frederick Douglass. Of the modest number of black Americans in 1968 wealthy enough to entertain in such grand style, some definitely would have lived in Washington.

They wouldn't have lived where the Jordans did, though. Chez Jordan is in one of the city's most expensive, most exclusive neighborhoods, a leafy enclave tucked next to Rock Creek Park. Forty years ago, the area would have been literally exclusive: By unassailable tradition, if not by binding legal covenant (such contracts had already been ruled null and void by the courts), the neighborhood would have been all white. That prohibition wouldn't have included the suspiciously swarthy foreign diplomat or two who might have occupied one of the official residences in the area; diplomatic immunity brought with it a kind of honorary whiteness. But even a credit-to-their-race Negro couple as educated, successful, and affluent as the Jordans wouldn't have lived in a mansion with a swimming pool on Embassy Row.

By 1968, well-to-do African American families had already begun an exodus from their old haunts in the neighborhoods around prestigious, historically black Howard University, perched on the escarpment that defined the original boundary of the city. The cultural and commercial soul of those areas, called Shaw and LeDroit Park, had been immolated in the riots that followed the assassination of the Reverend Martin Luther King Jr. in April of that year. The small, educated, moneyed black demographic that W. E. B. DuBois called the "Talented Tenth" was now more likely to be found along the graceful, tree-lined streets branching out from upper Sixteenth Street Northwest, the meridian that runs down the middle of the city like an arrow aimed at the portico of the White House. This latter-day Strivers' Row was and still is called the Gold Coast, although there's no nearby body of water except tiny Rock Creek. Houses there are spacious and impressive, though somewhat less so than the stately piles you see on Embassy Row.

So forty years ago there could have been a fancy dinner party in Washington hosted by an African American family in a big, elegant house, but the house would have been elsewhere in the city. Beyond this point, our thought experiment begins to break down.

For one thing, while most of the guests at Vernon and Ann Jordan's house that night were black, there were whites as well—Michael Lynton, the chairman of Sony Pictures, for example, and James A. Johnson, the longtime Democratic Party grandee who ran Fannie Mae before Raines did. While no one would claim that Washington social life is a model of integration today, four decades ago it was much more segregated. The best way to explain the difference is that in 1968 it would have been noteworthy if a society dinner was racially integrated, even in a token sense. In 2008, it would have been noteworthy if such an affair was not.

As for the political moment, always a relevant variable in assessing a Washington dinner party, there can be no comparison. It goes without saying that in 1968, the first African American had not just been elected president; the new occupant of the White House was one Richard Milhous Nixon.

There could have been no Valerie Jarrett to make her debut as a close friend and adviser to the new president. In fact, forty years ago there could have been no Valerie Jarrett at all—a princess of black Chicago (her grandfather was the first chief of the Chicago Housing Authority, her father a prominent physician, her ex-husband the son of a pioneering black journalist), whose history included stints as a behind-the-scenes operator in city government, a successful real estate developer, and the chair of the Chicago Stock Exchange. Black women of such pedigree were rare; black women with such résumés did not exist.

Nor would most of the other guests have existed. No African American had risen nearly as high in corporate America as Parsons or Raines. No African American ran a television network the way Lee did (or lived, as Lee did, just around the bend from the Jordans). No African American was waiting impatiently for his nomination as attorney general to be announced. As a general rule, only one black journalist at a time was taken seriously as a political pundit—exclusively on issues having to do with race. And black Washingtonians only got bold-faced treatment in the gossip columns of the *Afro-American* and other black newspapers, never in the mass-circulation *Washington Post* or *Evening Star.*

That lovely evening at the Jordans' never could have taken place without the disintegration of the black America we once knew. Some other aspects of disintegration, however, are much less salutary.

Two months later, when Obama was inaugurated, the band from Paul Laurence Dunbar High School marched in his parade. It was an occasion of great local pride, and not just because the school is located only a couple of miles from the Capitol: Dunbar, founded in 1870 as the Preparatory High School for Colored Youth, was the first public high school for African Americans in the nation.

It is hard to overstate what Dunbar High School meant to black America in the first half of the twentieth century. It was an elite institution, the place where the best and brightest young African Americans were taught that it wasn't enough to be as focused, determined, and accomplished as their white counterparts—they had to be better. Graduates included Dr. Charles R. Drew, the inventor of the modern blood bank; Charles Hamilton Houston, the legal scholar best known for his association with one of the young lawyers he mentored, Thurgood Marshall; the eminent poet Sterling Brown; and scores of other black pioneers. The faculty included the likes of Carter G. Woodson, the second African American to receive a PhD from Harvard (after W. E. B. DuBois) and the father of black history as a recognized academic discipline; and a music teacher named Henry Lee Grant, who found time to give after-hours lessons in the art and science of harmony to a promising young pianist named Edward Kennedy "Duke"

Ellington. Ambitious black parents would pick up and move to Washington so their children could attend Dunbar High.

That was then.

In 2008, more than half a century after the *Brown v. Board of Education* Supreme Court ruling desegregated the schools, Dunbar High's student body was 94 percent black; the remainder was mostly Hispanic. Less than 19 percent of Dunbar students were tested as "proficient" in reading and just 25 percent in math. Incredibly, given the school's history, not even 2 percent of the school's students qualified as "advanced" in either reading or math. Even more incredibly, this abysmal performance represented a modest *improvement* over the previous year.[8] At this rate, it will take Dunbar another half century to get back to where it started. On a school-evaluation website that solicits evaluations from students, one recent graduate called the onetime pearl of African American secondary education "just another ghetto school."

The Dunbar band looked and sounded great on inauguration day, though, thundering and high-stepping down Pennsylvania Avenue to celebrate a day that few black Americans imagined would ever come. It was a rare glimpse of the Abandoned during a week of self-congratulatory events that at times looked like a mandatory roll call of the Transcendent.

There was the party, for example, that BET's Lee threw at her home—a midcentury modernist classic that once was billionaire Jack Kent Cooke's pied-à-terre. Amid the Dale Chihuly glass sculptures and the sleek furniture by Mies van der Rohe and Breuer, there loomed Earvin "Magic" Johnson, the basketball legend who had become a multimillionaire with his shrewd cineplex and restaurant developments in black urban and suburban communities nationwide. He was chatting in the living room with his wife, Cookie; his mother sat on the couch next to the wife of Congressman James Clyburn of South Carolina, the majority whip in the House of Representatives and one of the most powerful men on Capitol Hill. Across the room full of luminaries from Hollywood, New York, Chicago, Atlanta, and Washington was Gayle King, the radio host best known as Oprah Winfrey's best friend, giving an account of an intimate dinner she and Winfrey had shared with Barack and Michelle Obama—just the four of them—a few days after the election.

Winfrey wasn't there that night, but she appeared two days later at a vast, glittering, black-tie party held in the Smithsonian's newly renovated National Museum of American History on the Mall. She was whisked right to the VIP room, of course, but other celebrities mingled with the hoi polloi—Samuel L. Jackson, Spike Lee, all the usual-suspect media luminaries, plus the odd Hollywood ingenue or Wall Street venture capitalist.

Also present at the museum party was Harvard's "Skip" Gates, the most famous black academic superstar in the country and perhaps the world. A few months later, he would give the nation an object lesson in the new, uncharted realities of a disintegrated black America.

* * *

Six months into his term, the first African American president of the United States was giving what was a fairly boring and predictable news conference—until Barack Obama volunteered that police had acted "stupidly" in handcuffing, arresting, and tossing in jail his friend Skip Gates.

A story that had been simmering for days suddenly boiled over. Gates, feeling unwell, had been returning from an exhausting trip to China in connection with a new documentary he was making for PBS. He was met at the airport by his regular driver, a man of North African descent who worked for a local car service. The town car pulled up at Gates's house near the Harvard campus—as one of the most lauded faculty members at the nation's most prestigious university, Gates was accorded the perk of living in Harvard-owned housing. He has a disability and walks with a cane, so the driver helped him carry his bags to the house. To his annoyance, Gates found that the front door was jammed; neither he nor the driver could open it, so he went around to the back and let himself in. He and the driver began working on the front door from the inside and managed to get it open.

A passerby had been watching as two men carrying bags arrived at a house in one of Cambridge's most expensive and exclusive neighborhoods, tried to force the front door, and then headed around to the back. Understandably, she called the police and told them what she had seen.

Sergeant James Crowley, who is white, responded to the call. By the time he got there, Gates was already in his house. Crowley demanded that Gates identify himself, and Gates—weary, cranky, and now, from his point of view, hassled—went semi-ballistic. He protested that he was in his own house. He accused Crowley of harassing him because of his race. He pulled rank, at one point telling the Cambridge police sergeant: "You have no idea who you're messing with."

Crowley satisfied himself that Gates was in his own home, that there had been no burglary, and that no one was in any peril. Then, as Gates walked out onto the front porch—still giving the officer some lip—Crowley arrested him for disorderly conduct, handcuffed him, and took him down to the station, where he was booked and put into a cell. He was soon released, and within days all charges were dropped.

It should have been a teachable moment, but few seemed to understand the lesson: For both men, this was a new power dynamic.

Crowley wrote in his police report that the complaining witness had told him she saw two "black men" acting suspiciously at the house, when in fact she hadn't specified race at all. This suggests that Crowley arrived on the scene with a bag full of assumptions. Nowhere among them was the notion of a Transcendent black man who towered above him in affluence, education, status, and power—and who acted that way.

Crowley had spent more than twenty years on the Cambridge police force; encountering a rock-star Harvard professor who happens to be arrogant is like meeting a professional basketball player who happens to be tall. This can't have been the first time a Harvard grandee had treated Crowley like a lesser species. Yet there was something about Gates's uppitiness that led the police sergeant to arrest a fifty-eight-year-old man who stands five seven, walks with a cane, and without question was in his own house.

But Gates, too, was in unfamiliar territory. It's as if he didn't fully appreciate the noblesse oblige requirements of his Transcendent status. He immediately assumed the defiant posture of the underdog, the disenfranchised, the powerless, when in fact he is a card-carrying member of today's Establishment. He obviously felt that he couldn't give an inch to Crowley, and I believe that's because many successful African Americans, even Transcendents, secretly worry that somehow their gains are all precarious. I think that at some level Gates feared that while today he might be a rich and famous Harvard professor, tomorrow he could be just another black man trying to make his way in a hostile and discriminatory world.

Even Obama read the situation wrong. He approached it with a Transcendent mind-set, assuming that everyone would understand why such a high-status black man might react, or overreact, the way Gates did. Not everyone understood. The president's reaction took account of the historical baggage that even the most successful African Americans carry around—the sensitivity to perceived racial slights, along with the suspicion that there are whites who resent the success of African Americans. To some whites, however, Obama's words came across not as a dispassionate analysis of the incident but as an expression of racial solidarity. The thing is, Obama was right: Pretty much by definition, arresting a nonthreatening man on his own front porch for being in a bad mood is a pretty stupid thing for a police officer to do. But Obama had to apologize and invite everybody for a beer.

The story became a "talker" precisely because it was such a familiar scenario—white cop, black suspect—with such an unfamiliar power relationship. It's as if the laws of societal physics had changed, as if a basic formula like $F = ma$ no longer worked the way it had for Newton or Einstein.

* * *

This book is an exploration of the new social and demographic landscape in a disintegrated black America, and the implications for the larger society. It grew out of a talk I gave several years ago, what was supposed to be a five-minute address to a group of black publishing executives. I had been thinking about black America and its increasing incoherence, at least for me, as a useful conceptual framework.

It seemed to me that one size no longer fit all. We could talk about the need to increase black academic achievement in the poorest neighborhoods of Atlanta and the need to increase black academic achievement in the comfortable suburb of Lithonia, for example, but the problems aren't the same and the solutions wouldn't be the same. We could pretend not to notice how distinctive African immigrants are from native-born black Americans, or we could try to understand those differences and put them in context. We could continue to accept the one-drop rule mandating that anyone with any discernible African heritage was black, period, end of story, or we could remember that the rule was imposed on us in the context of slavery and Jim Crow and decide to look under the rug to see what we could find. We could not, it seemed to me, expect to convince anyone that all of black America still suffered equally from its unique history, not when black Americans were plainly visible in positions of supreme power and influence. It was increasingly clear to me that there was no one black America—that there were several, and that we had to distinguish among them if we were to talk intelligently about African Americans in the twenty-first century.

It was also clear to me that not everyone would immediately warm to this idea. Unity has always been a powerful weapon in African Americans' struggle for freedom, justice, and equality. Solidarity was essential; the privileged few could not, and would not, sell out the underprivileged many. Anything that divided us could only weaken us; and since others would surely try to split us apart, we could at least vow not to do their dirty work for them. I was raised to honor and cherish this ethic of absolute, unquestioned, unqualified African American unity. Then again, that was some time ago.

I decided to broach this touchy subject in my remarks to the publishing executives. What happened next was a complete surprise: My audience reacted immediately with such engagement and enthusiasm that my scheduled drive-by greeting turned into an animated, intense, hour-long dialogue.

These black professionals—all members of the Mainstream—didn't just want to hear my ideas about the disintegration of black America; they wanted to tell me about their own experiences and explain their own views. Several chimed in to reinforce the idea that a gap has opened between an educated, middle-class black America and a poor, uneducated black America. Some said they saw the gap becoming ever larger and lamented the growing separation. "And you haven't mentioned the African immigrants," one listener offered. And from another: "There are more people who are mixed race, and they're causing us to redefine what it means to be black."

I began poring through census data, marketing studies, and any other material I thought might help advance my thinking or turn it around. Eventually some of this research surfaced in my *Washington Post* column. A piece entitled "Which Black America?" included these passages:

> Why does the National Urban League, an organization
> for which I have great respect, compile its annual
> "State of Black America" report in a way that makes the
> condition of African Americans seem both better and
> worse than it really is?

Trying to encompass all of black America in a few easily grasped numbers is far from a meaningless exercise. But it doesn't point the way toward specific policies for different segments of a diverse population.

Why has the NAACP, once such a potent force, lost so much of its membership and relevance? I would argue that it's because the organization continues to look for a "black agenda" around which we can all unite with the fervor and passion of decades past, when in fact there's a need for multiple agendas.[9]

These observations got me an off-the-record cussing out by one of the elders of the civil rights struggle, who thought I had taken cheap shots at two historic freedom-fighting organizations that had made my life and career possible. I was sorry that anyone took the column that way. But it also inspired hundreds of e-mails, most of them supportive (or at least polite), and it electrified the weekly discussion I host on washingtonpost.com. What struck me was how rarely anyone rejected my ideas out of hand as some kind of betrayal of historical unity. Much more common was a desire to move forward, to find contemporary language for contemporary conditions, to frame our search for effective policies—and constructive individual actions—in terms of how things are rather than how they were. Some callers and e-mailers demanded to know why, in their view, I'd pulled my punches. Why hadn't I been more critical of the National Urban League, always so brainy and analytical, for not being more incisive about the disintegrative process that was so obviously taking place? And why hadn't I slammed the NAACP for wasting its time on symbolic gestures, like a mock funeral to bury the word "nigger," when historic changes were taking place in the real world?

With no offense to the NAACP, which is now under new leadership, such symbolic gestures seem particularly lame in the face of the Obama presidency. Suddenly objective reality is plenty profound: After nearly four hundred years of struggle that commenced when the first African slaves were brought ashore at Jamestown, a black man was freely elected president of the United States—and a black family moved into the White House. Psychologists can search all they want for combinations of words and images that penetrate the chamber of our collective subconscious labeled "race," and still they won't do better than the network-television crews that follow the president wherever he goes, cameras rolling as he motorcades to a summit or helicopters to Camp David. One of Obama's early acts was to issue the traditional proclamation making February Black History Month, and the irony was inescapable. As president, he had just assumed the role of History-Maker in Chief. The nation was going to have to acknowledge that *every* month is Black History Month.

Perhaps, for the first time, it is impossible for anyone to escape the fact that the black American experience is nothing more or less than an integral and necessary component of the American experience. In the summer of 2008, as the Obama campaign churned along, the writer, scholar, and MacArthur Foundation "genius" grant winner Charles Johnson published an article in *The American Scholar* titled "The End of the Black American Narrative." He posited that a "unique black American narrative, which emphasizes the experience of victimization, is quietly in the background of every conversation we have about black people, even when it is not fully articulated or expressed. It is our starting point, our agreed-upon premise, our most important presupposition for dialogues about black America." This narrative is based on "group victimization," Johnson writes, and it is obsolete; it blinds us to "the inevitability of change"—and the fact of change.[10] His argument is deliberately provocative, and I believe it goes too far; he seems ready to dismiss race as almost irrelevant in today's America, while I believe its relevance is changed and diminished but still clearly palpable. Someday, perhaps, I won't worry that my two middle-class, educated, young-adult sons run the risk of being unfairly pulled over by police for "driving while black," or that the ensuing interaction with the police officer is disproportionately likely to spin tragically out of control. Until then, I'm convinced that race still matters, even if it matters less.

But Johnson is onto something when he argues that a single black narrative no longer applies—if it ever did—and that heterogeneity of class and culture are as much a feature of black America as they are of the rest of America. He is also right when he says that it is time to look at black America—I would say the four black Americas—with a clear and critical eye.

To find out where we are, we have to trace where we've been. There was a time before disintegration, a time before integration. So let us turn now to the era of segregation, a system designed to oppress and demean—and a time African Americans made much more of than we sometimes give ourselves credit for.

2 WHEN WE WERE ONE

The wooded hills around Atlanta boast some of the wealthiest black-majority suburbs in the country, sylvan tracts where cavernous McMansions line emerald-green golf courses and the relatively disadvantaged are marked by their puny entry-level BMWs and Benzes. It's no exaggeration to say that the city whose destruction was so lavishly lamented by Scarlett O'Hara and Rhett Butler in *Gone with the Wind* has become, in the early years of the twenty-first century, the closest thing to an authentic mecca for the black middle class. Thirty or forty years ago, upwardly mobile African Americans were all about making their way to Washington, D.C., also known as Chocolate City, a place of seemingly limitless possibility for the young, gifted, and black. Now the preferred destination is Atlanta—the ATL in the argot of hip-hop culture, of which Atlanta is a nexus—and nobody stops to think of the irony: Wasn't the idea to get *away* from Tara?

In the years following the civil rights movement, when Atlanta was struggling to shed its Old South historical identity and become a hub of the modern world, boosters called it "The

City Too Busy to Hate." A hundred years ago, however, hate was the main event. Black Atlanta was under an assault no less relentless than the scorched-earth campaign waged decades earlier by General William Tecumseh Sherman, but not nearly so well known—a campaign of terror against African Americans, with a climax that isn't mentioned, for some reason, in the slick promotional materials handed out by the Atlanta Convention and Visitors Bureau. Back then, the story of race in Atlanta mostly centered on a swath of more or less contiguous neighborhoods south of the city's busy center—the University Center District, Sweet Auburn, Brownsville, and Darktown—and was largely defined by white Atlanta's white-hot revanchist rage.

By 1906, the systematic disenfranchisement of African Americans in the states of the former Confederacy was well under way. Then, as now, Atlanta was the economic and cultural heart of something called the "New South." Henry Grady, a prominent journalist, orator, and eventual co-owner of the *Atlanta Constitution*, had coined the term a decade after the Civil War to herald his vision of a reborn South, literally risen from the ashes of Sherman's apocalypse—a New South in which the old order was reestablished, with whites as masters and blacks as their laborers and servants. The 1877 removal of the last federal troops from the South, along with the 1883 Supreme Court ruling in the so-called Civil Rights Cases that allowed states to enforce Jim Crow laws, put an end to the false spring of Reconstruction. For black people in Atlanta, the air turned bitter cold. A poll tax was imposed. Mixing in theaters, on streetcars, and at public parks was outlawed. Atlanta moved toward becoming the most segregated city in the South, its code of strict separation, white dominance, and black subservience enforced by all-too-frequent lynchings.

The same thing was happening throughout the South: the virtual re-enslavement of African Americans and a return to what racists like Grady considered the "natural" order of things. Nowhere was this bitter pill more difficult for black people to swallow than in Atlanta, where the former slaves and their descendants had come so far. There, a critical mass of black ambition had ignited what seemed an unstoppable reaction. Black educational institutions such as Atlanta University and Morehouse College were producing an educated elite. Black businesses, while still small in relative terms, were expanding and producing real economic benefits for the whole African American community. The grand project of black uplift looked so promising; now it was being snuffed out. In Atlanta, which was the intellectual center of black America, prominent thinkers waged a vital debate: What could black people do about this brutal campaign to kill the black American dream?

It was in Atlanta's Piedmont Park, during the Cotton States and International Exposition of 1895, that Booker T. Washington gave his famous—or infamous—"Atlanta Compromise" speech. He was willing for "the race" to indefinitely postpone its demands for full equality; in exchange, he demanded only the chance for African Americans to make slow, steady economic and educational progress. Once black people were sufficiently prepared, he believed, the barriers that now confined them would simply fall away.

To the white citizens of Atlanta, Washington offered soothing reassurance:

[You] can be sure in the future, as in the past, that you and your families will be surrounded by the most patient, faithful, law-abiding, and unresentful people that the world has seen. As we have proved our loyalty to you in the past, in nursing your children, watching by the sick-bed of your mothers and fathers, and often following them with tear-dimmed eyes to their graves, so in the future, in our humble way, we shall stand by you with a devotion that no foreigner can approach, ready to lay down our lives, if need be, in defense of yours.

And to black Atlantans, a warning not to get too uppity:

The wisest among my race understand that the agitation of questions of social equality is the extremest folly, and that progress in the enjoyment of all the privileges that will come to us must be the result of severe and constant struggle rather than of artificial forcing. No race that has anything to contribute to the markets of the world is long in any degree ostracized. It is important and right that all privileges of the law be ours, but it is vastly more important that we be prepared for the exercise of these privileges. The opportunity to earn a dollar in a factory just now is worth infinitely more than the opportunity to spend a dollar in an opera-house.[1]

The other side of the argument was represented by W. E. B. DuBois, the brilliant black scholar who would later be remembered as one of the founders of the National Association for the Advancement of Colored People (NAACP). A Northerner who moved to Atlanta to take a professorship at Atlanta University, DuBois initially had favorable things to say about the "Atlanta Compromise," partly out of respect for Washington and his position as the most powerful and influential black man in the country. Soon, though, DuBois lost both his patience and his tolerance for any kind of compromise: "Mr. Washington represents in Negro thought the old attitude of adjustment and submission," he wrote in *The Souls of Black Folk*, his landmark 1903 book of essays. "[His] programme practically accepts the alleged inferiority of the Negro races."

DuBois continued:

Mr. Washington distinctly asks that black people give up, at least for the present, three things—

First, political power,

Second, insistence on civil rights,

Third, higher education of Negro youth,

—and concentrate all their energies on industrial education, and accumulation of wealth, and the conciliation of the South. This policy has been courageously and insistently advocated for over fifteen years, and has been triumphant for perhaps ten years. As a result of this tender of the palm-branch, what has been the return? In these years there have occurred:

1. The disfranchisement of the Negro.

2. The legal creation of a distinct status of civil inferiority for the Negro.

3. The steady withdrawal of aid from institutions for the higher training of the Negro.

These movements are not, to be sure, direct results of Mr. Washington's teachings; but his propaganda has, without a shadow of doubt, helped their speedier accomplishment.[2]

The debate, for the moment, was academic: Jim Crow marched relentlessly through the South, regardless of what black intellectuals might have to say about it. In Atlanta, the black entrepreneurs who had prospered during the boom years of the city's fin-de-siècle renaissance were forced to retreat from the bustling central business district and consolidate in segregated enclaves, especially along Auburn Avenue—Sweet Auburn—which *Fortune* magazine in 1956 called "the richest Negro street in the world," a mile and a half of black affluence. Like Harlem's Strivers' Row or Washington's LeDroit Park, Sweet Auburn became an important focal point of a new and growing phenomenon: the black middle class.

To the west of the Auburn Avenue neighborhood, a unique complex of African American educational institutions was being assembled—Morehouse College for men and Spelman College for women, Clark College, Morris Brown College, Atlanta University. If Sweet Auburn was black America's most powerful economic engine, the University Center District was its most dynamic intellectual center. At the eastern end of Sweet Auburn lay a sprawling, dirt-poor, all-black slum known as Darktown—one of scores of black ghettoes across the nation known by that generic name. The economic and social disparities among black Atlantans were clear for all to see, but at the time everyone assumed that eventually these gaps would become irrelevant. Ultimately, the rising tide of uplift would benefit all.

The few black Atlantans who were rich and the many who were poor had something in common, after all, that trumped any differences in wealth or education: They were all black, and white Atlantans were increasingly determined to keep them on the black side of town—and to do so "by any means necessary," as Malcolm X would say decades later in a very different context. There was nothing subtle about this campaign to put "colored" folks in their place and keep them there. In the summer of 1906, for example, a leading Georgia politician, Hoke Smith, issued what had become a typical warning: "We will control the Negro peacefully if we can—but with guns if we must."

On September 20, 1906, a white woman named Knowles Kimmel—a farmer's wife who would come to represent the flower of Southern womanhood—made a shocking claim. While she was alone at the Kimmel farmhouse, in a western Atlanta suburb known as Oakland City, a "strange, rough-looking Negro" had appeared out of nowhere and sexually assaulted her, she said. The assault, if it indeed took place, was built into a cause célèbre by the race-baiting Atlanta newspapers. The idea of sexually rapacious black men defiling innocent, defenseless white women was uniquely powerful—and, to white supremacists like Henry Grady and Hoke Smith, uniquely useful in radicalizing and mobilizing white public opinion.

Sensationalized reports about the Kimmel incident helped ignite a conflagration that turned out to be one of the most pivotal, least-remembered milestones in the history of race relations in the United States. In 1908, a muckraking New York journalist named Ray Stannard Baker—a contemporary and colleague of legends such as Ida Tarbell and Lincoln Steffens—published a groundbreaking book, *Following the Color Line: An Account of Negro Citizenship in the American Democracy.* In the first chapter, he told the story of what happened on September 22, 1906, when Atlanta reached its flashpoint:

And finally on this hot Saturday half-holiday, when the country people had come in by hundreds, when everyone was out of doors, when the streets were crowded, when the saloons had been filled since early morning with white men and Negroes, both drinking—certain newspapers in Atlanta began to print extras with big headings announcing new assaults on white women by Negroes. The Atlanta *News* published five such extras, and newsboys cried them through the city:

"Third assault."

"Fourth assault."

The whole city, already deeply agitated, was thrown into a veritable state of panic. The news in the extras was taken as truthful; for the city was not in a mood then for cool investigation.[3]

By the time his book was published, Baker had thoroughly investigated the alleged incidents. "Two of them may have been attempts at assaults," he wrote, "but two palpably were nothing more than fright on the part of both the white woman and the Negro. As an instance, in one case an elderly woman, Mrs. Martha Holcombe, going to close her blinds in the evening, saw a Negro on the sidewalk. In a terrible fright she screamed. The news was telephoned to the police station, but before the officials could respond, Mrs. Holcombe telephoned them not to come out. And yet this was one of the 'assaults' chronicled in letters five inches high in a newspaper extra."[4]

But white Atlantans were in a mood to believe the worst. White mobs began to gather, and they were well-armed, liberally inebriated, and hell-bent on revenge. Black Atlanta came under all-out attack.

White rioters pillaged black businesses, sometimes aiming for specific targets but settling for what was available. A mob smashed its way into a barbershop looking for the proprietor, Alonzo Herndon, a former slave who had become a wealthy businessman with extensive real estate holdings, a stake in an insurance company, and three profitable barbershops. When the mob arrived, Herndon had left for the day and the shop was closed. Momentarily disappointed, the rioters simply crossed the street to another barbershop—an establishment that had nothing at all to do with Herndon—where they smashed the place up, and, for good measure, killed all the barbers.

The whites continued their rampage through Atlanta's black neighborhoods for three days and nights. Crowded, bustling Decatur Street, with its black restaurants and saloons, was perhaps the epicenter, but black Atlantans were not truly safe anywhere in the city. A century later, the death toll remains unclear. Estimates of the number of blacks killed range from twenty-five to more than one hundred; most scholars agree that only two whites died, one of them from a heart attack.

DuBois wrote an anguished poem about the riot called "A Litany of Atlanta." One stanza goes:

A city lay in travail, God our Lord, and from her loins sprang twin Murder and Black Hate. Red was the midnight; clang, crack and cry of death and fury filled the air and trembled underneath the stars when church spires pointed silently to Thee. And all this was to sate the greed of greedy men who hide behind the veil of vengeance!

Bend us Thine ear, O Lord![5]

DuBois's stature rose in the wake of the Atlanta Race Riot of 1906. Support among black Americans for Booker T. Washington's accommodationist strategy declined. And the movement toward absolute separation of the races throughout the South became complete.

In Atlanta, the riot gave new impetus to the effort to shove black residents and businesses into segregated neighborhoods south and east of downtown—Sweet Auburn, Brownsville, University Central District, and the Old Fourth Ward on the east side, encompassing what once was Darktown. As Baker noted, "After the riot was over many Negro families, terrified and feeling themselves unprotected, sold out for what they could get—I heard a good many pitiful stories of such sudden and costly sacrifices—and left the country, some going to California, some to Northern cities."[6]

Baker's *Following the Color Line* quotes a letter from a young black man who joined the post-riot exodus out of Atlanta:

> . . . It is possible that you have formed at least a good idea of how we feel as the result of the horrible eruption in Georgia. I have not spoken to a Caucasian on the subject since then. But, listen: How would you feel, if with our history, there came a time when, after speeches and papers and teachings you acquired property and were educated, and were a fairly good man, it were impossible for you to walk the street (for whose maintenance you were taxed) with your sister without being in mortal fear of death if you resented any insult offered to her? How would you feel if you saw a governor, a mayor, a sheriff, whom you could not oppose at the polls, encourage by deed or word or

both, a mob of "best" and worst citizens to slaughter
your people in the streets and in their own homes
and in their places of business? Do you think that you
could resist the same wrath that caused God to slay
the Philistines and the Russians to throw bombs? I can
resist it, but with each new outrage I am less able to
resist it. And yet if I gave way to my feelings I should
become just like other men . . . of the mob![7]

The full psychological impact of the Atlanta riot may be
incalculable, but one specific result is clear. Many whites—
even those who disapproved of mob violence, lynching, and
the terrorism of the Ku Klux Klan—were deeply shaken by the
many instances during the melee in which blacks displayed
the will and the means to fight back. Segregationists pointed
to the resistance as proof that they were right—that blacks had
to be kept down, had to be kept in their place. Measures to
deny black citizens the vote throughout the South were per-
fected. Public accommodations were labeled whites only and
blacks only; merchants began requiring black patrons to enter
through the back door. This whole blueprint for the New South
was codified into law as a way of delineating two ostensibly
"separate but equal" societies. Black Atlanta was effectively
walled off from the rest of the city, left to make its own way in
the world. The long, dark night of Jim Crow segregation had
fallen.

* * *

Jim Crow was bad in the cities of the South, but in small towns
and rural areas it was all but intolerable. The system of share-

cropping that tied many families to the land and mired them in poverty was almost as oppressive as slavery. There was no question of voting rights or fair treatment by the courts. The Klan was in its heyday, and blacks impertinent enough to demand to be treated as full citizens ran a very real risk of being lynched—the whole point of Klan-style terrorism was to make examples of "troublemakers" so that everyone else would stay in line. Black schools were kept inferior by design, which meant parents could not even dream that the next generation would have a better life. Faced with such a hopeless situation, many African Americans just packed up and left.

They went north, seeking prosperity and freedom, in a series of waves known collectively as the Great Migration. You could plot their destinations by following the routes of the nearest rail lines—families from North and South Carolina settled in Washington, Baltimore, Philadelphia, Pittsburgh, Newark, Boston; those from Alabama, Mississippi, and Georgia tended to end up in Chicago, Cincinnati, Cleveland, St. Louis, Kansas City, Detroit; and many migrants from Texas and Louisiana headed west to Los Angeles, San Francisco, Oakland, and Seattle. New York City, as usual, was a magnet for newcomers from all over. Between 1910 and 1940, an estimated 1.6 million black Americans from the South moved north and west; between 1940 and 1970, another five million followed. Their impact could hardly have been more transformative. In Chicago, for example, African Americans went from 2 percent of the city's population in 1910 to 33 percent in 1970.[8]

The migrants found jobs in the steel mills of Gary, the shipyards of Philadelphia, the automobile factories of Flint, the meat-packing plants of Kansas City. They found better schools for their children and escape from the threat of terrorists in white robes. What they didn't find, for the most part, was anything like the Valhalla of racial integration and harmony that many had expected.

On one level, the newly arrived African Americans were just like the other hyphenated ethnic groups that had arrived in their turn—except, of course, they didn't use hyphens in those days. The Irish, the Italians, and the Poles were not yet assimilated, and they saw black newcomers from the South as competitors for jobs—and later, after the newcomers were settled, for political patronage. In that sense, African Americans were just another ethnic clan. As had been the routine with the other clans, new arrivals gravitated toward neighborhoods where a support system was already in place: relatives or acquaintances from the same Southern town who could offer temporary lodgings; a job or at least the rumor of employment; the phone number of someone who might know someone who could open the right doors; the possibility of making quick friendships with experienced city dwellers who knew the ropes. But these reasons only partly explain why blacks ended up in segregated enclaves like Harlem in New York City or Bronzeville in Chicago. There was, and is, something stubbornly powerful about race as a dividing line.

Chicago, to take perhaps the clearest example, was a young city with no history of slavery or Jim Crow—a city whose first nonindigenous settler had been Jean Baptiste Point du Sable, a black man. Illinois had progressive laws that outlawed segregation in education and public accommodations. Yet blacks were confined to the sprawling South Side through a web of racially restrictive housing covenants that put most fashionable North Side neighborhoods off-limits. In other words, the private sector did what the public sector would not. The South

Side eventually grew to become—and remains today—the biggest and most populous black-majority neighborhood in the country.

To be sure, there were exceptions. My father, Harold I. Robinson, was a statistic in the Great Migration. He was born in 1916 in Canon, Georgia, a small town in the northeast part of the state. This was during a relatively brief stopover in the family's journey north, which took years to complete; each of his five siblings was born in a different city. They made it all the way to Michigan and settled in Ann Arbor—then, as now, a liberal-minded college town whose views on social issues were radically ahead of their time. My father attended integrated Ann Arbor High School, then went on to study at the University of Michigan and earn his law degree at Wayne State University in Detroit. An African American man whose entire secondary and postsecondary education came at integrated institutions was a great rarity.

Still, when he was called to serve his country in World War II my father was relegated to racially segregated units. The friends of his that I met from his Michigan years were African American. Even with his atypical background, he grew up with a profound sense of himself as a black man who belonged to a black community that was not allowed to participate fully in the social, political, and economic life of its country—a community that had to construct a social, political, and economic life of its own.

That was the case throughout the country. It's true that racial segregation in the South, enforced by law and terror, wasn't the same as racial segregation in the North and West, which was often enforced by housing covenants but also had to do with custom and clan. It's true that the hybrid segregation in a city like Washington, caught between North and South, was different from either system in its purest form. But whatever the formalities, it can be said that for most of the twentieth-century black Americans lived in mostly black or all-black neighborhoods and towns—a beige, tan, and brown archipelago of humanity constituting a separate "nation" that could meaningfully be called "black America."

Today, that once-indivisible nation persists in memory, imagination, and discourse—but not in the real world.

* * *

When I was growing up in the late 1950s and early 1960s, my own private black America was essentially a college town. Orangeburg, South Carolina, is home to two historically black colleges, Claflin University and South Carolina State University, which sit side by side just a couple of hundred yards from the house, built by my great-grandfather, where I grew up. My mother, Louisa S. Robinson, was head librarian at Claflin for decades; my father taught at the school for a time; my great-aunt, who lived with us, was at various times head nurse at both schools. The Claflin and SCSU campuses were as familiar to me as my own backyard. Orangeburg, with a "metropolitan" population of around fifteen thousand, was said to be home to more black PhDs per capita than any other city or town in the nation. Indeed, most of the adults I knew were associated with either Claflin or SCSU, and so many of them had advanced degrees that I remember hearing the grown folks gossip about the father of one of my good friends: What was wrong with the man, people whispered, that it was taking him so long to earn his doctorate?

From first grade through junior high I attended Felton Training School, which was housed on the SCSU campus in an old Rosenwald schoolhouse. There's a story behind that building and thousands like it. In 1912, Booker T. Washington approached Julius Rosenwald, the president of Sears, Roebuck and Co., with a request. Rosenwald was a philanthropist who had given money to Washington's Tuskegee Institute, and Washington wanted permission to use some of the funds to build six simple schoolhouses in rural Alabama to serve black communities where educational facilities were either substandard or nonexistent. Rosenwald agreed, and after the schools were built he was so proud of the results that he formed a foundation to build schoolhouses for black students throughout the South. By 1928, one of every three rural and small-town black students in the Southern states was learning in a Rosenwald schoolhouse. Rosenwald had architects develop standard floor plans and elevations, depending on how large a building was needed and which direction it faced—the buildings were designed with big windows to take maximum advantage of natural light. Felton was built in 1925 according to "Floor Plan 400"—a "four-teacher community school" meant to be situated facing east or west. Each of the four classrooms housed two grades, and each of the four teachers—Mrs. Clinkscales, Mrs. White, Mrs. Edwards, and Mrs. Lewis—was skilled enough and formidable enough to teach two classes of unruly children at the same time.

Just before I graduated, officials at SCSU decided to build a low-slung, modern-style "new Felton"—better in every way as an educational facility, but lacking the old Felton's history and soul. This was before the concept of historic preservation had fully penetrated the national consciousness, and the old Rosenwald building was promptly razed. When the Democratic Party held its first presidential debate of the 2008 campaign at SCSU, the anchor desk for MSNBC, where I was doing commentary, was just yards from where the old Felton had stood. Chris Matthews and the rest of my colleagues must have wondered why I kept gazing at the parking lot across the street rather than at the camera, and why my eyes kept tearing up.

The families of many Felton students had something to do with one or the other of the two colleges. I also had classmates, however, whose parents were farmers or merchants. Not one of the Felton families was truly rich but most were comfortable; a few were poor. What we had in common was being black.

The same was true of my neighborhood not far from downtown, where a fifty-yard radius would have encompassed the homes of a teacher, a professor, a cobbler, and a clerk. Likewise at Trinity Methodist Church, which we attended every Sunday: Some families were relatively better off and some relatively worse off, some better-educated than others. There were indeed social and economic class divisions in the black America of my childhood, and I recognized them at the time—it was obvious that my life was different from the lives of the kids growing up in Sunnyside, a neighborhood of shotgun shacks where abject poverty and noxious dysfunction were evident for all to see. But it was a given that the factors that might have divided us were far outweighed by a single attribute that both defined and united us: We were all black, and to be black was to live under assault. That was just the way things were. It didn't matter how well you might have been dressed or how many college degrees you might have had. If a restaurant didn't offer service to "colored" people, you weren't going to eat there. If the city built a new whites-only playground, you kept out. If a redneck in a pickup truck wanted to yell "Nigger!" at the first black person he saw, you were eligible.

I don't want to give the wrong impression. I think of my childhood as idyllic, and it never would have occurred to either my sister, Ellen, or me to entertain the notion that the South's system of white hegemony had anything to do with intelligence, ability, or merit. If anything, our environment suggested the opposite: The black Orangeburg we knew was cultured, well-traveled, and urbane, while the white Orangeburg we saw around us—basically a commercial depot and service center for an agricultural belt—seemed unlettered and uncouth. When I left Felton and went to the newly integrated Orangeburg High, which previously had been the whites-only high school in town—I learned that some white people were better than I had thought and some were worse. But the point is that never for a moment was I confused about which "side" I was on, and never would I have imagined that I had the slightest choice in the matter.

In the North, of course, black people did not have to endure all the Jim Crow insults and indignities that we suffered in the South. But those émigré African Americans also were denied acceptance as full participants in the great American experiment. They lived, for the most part, in all-black neighborhoods. They were not welcome at many universities—Princeton, for example, mistakenly admitted its first African American undergraduate in 1935, promptly kicked him out after discovering he was black, and then allowed no more black students until forced to do so by the navy in 1942 as part of the war effort. Blacks in the North were not hired at many worksites, not granted raises or promotions that they deserved, not welcomed into many white neighborhoods, not given access to the credit they would need to grow small businesses into big ones. They asked for the chance to fight for their country in two world wars and were made to serve in all-black units and perform some of the most unpleasant or dangerous tasks— collecting the bodies from the Normandy beaches after D-day, for example. My father believed his lungs were permanently damaged from working in a chemical munitions facility during the war. My father-in-law, Edward Rhodes Collins, had the ridiculously dangerous assignment of manning an ammunition ship in the South Pacific.

The key thing was that we were *all* in that ammo boat together, metaphorically speaking. Racial apartheid, imposed and enforced by others, ironically had fostered great cohesion among African Americans, binding together social and economic classes that otherwise might have drifted apart. One unintended impact of laws and customs mandating racial segregation was to create, within black America, a remarkable state of *integration*.

What was this separate but integrated black America like? I lived through what Dick Cheney might have called the "last throes" of Jim Crow, and even though my memories are vivid it's hard to recapture what it really felt like—the constant tension and stomach-churning anxiety that came with the status of being, officially, a second-class citizen. Here's just one episode: My family was out for a Sunday drive, and my grandmother, who would have been in her late seventies, needed to use the bathroom. My father pulled over at a gas station—it was always risky to stop at a gas station you hadn't patronized in the past, but sometimes you had no choice—and the good old boy at the cash register directed my grandmother past the restrooms labeled MEN and WOMEN, all the way around to the back of the building where there was a dank, smelly toilet labeled COLORED. This was after segregation in public accommodations had been made illegal, but civil rights laws and Supreme Court decisions had little weight in the benighted towns and hamlets of rural South Carolina. I remember my grandmother's look of shame—she had a simple human need and was being treated as if she were less than human, and she didn't have the option of doing the dignified thing, which would have been to walk away. I remember my father's anger—he glowered and grumbled and vowed to write a letter of complaint to the chairman of Esso. I don't know if he eventually wrote the letter, but even if he had managed to deprive one backwoods racist of a livelihood he didn't deserve, at some level my father must have felt hopelessly impotent. He must have known that although sending a letter was the most effective thing he could do—basically, the only thing he could do—it wasn't nearly enough. In those days, you had to wonder if anything would ever be enough. He must have felt not just anger but powerlessness, not just rage but inadequacy.

So it's important not to view the past through a fog of sepia-toned nostalgia. No one who values liberty, quality, opportunity, or justice—no one, really, who values the ideals for which this country is supposed to stand—would actually want to turn back the clock.

That said, however, there must be some reason why black Americans were so much more optimistic forty years ago than they are today, as is demonstrably the case. In 1969, when African American survey respondents were asked "Are blacks better off than five years ago?" around 70 percent said yes, according to the Pew Research Center. When that question was put to African Americans in 2007, only 20 percent said yes[9]—meaning, at the very least, that the confident sense of unimpeded ascent that so many black Americans felt forty years ago had all but disappeared. Since that recent polling was done prior to the election of the first African American president, it's unclear what effect the dawning of the age of Obama has had on attitudes. It's likely that black Americans have rediscovered some of their old optimism, but it's unlikely that they've reclaimed all of it. The past forty years have seen so many advances for African Americans—higher incomes, better housing, new opportunities for education and employment, meaningful participation in the civic and political life of the nation, the opening of myriad doors that once seemed hermetically sealed against people of color. So why the sense that while all this was gained, something valuable was slipping away? And what was that "something" that we lost?

* * *

Imagine a typical urban scene from an old black-and-white movie—streetcars, newspaper hawkers, the men in suits and fedoras, the women with their hair done in elaborate swoops, waves, and curls. Now imagine that everyone in the scene is black, and you have an idea of what midcentury black America was like.

The 1906 riot in Atlanta greatly sped up the process of segregation, and soon the lines of racial demarcation were fixed: whites had their neighborhoods on the north side of the city and blacks had theirs on the south side. During working hours, there was plenty of mixing—whites needed blacks as labor; many blacks relied on white employers for their livelihoods. After dark and on weekends, though, everyone understood who belonged where. If a black man wanted to take a Sunday stroll, he knew enough not to promenade on the white side of town.

What evolved on the south side of town was a community that of necessity was socially, culturally, and economically integrated—a development mirrored in cities throughout the country, though rarely as vividly. There were two factors that made black Atlanta in the pre–civil rights era something of a special case: The city was the "Hub of the South," centrally located in the region where African Americans were most heavily concentrated; and the complex of historically black educational institutions served as a magnet to draw the best and brightest from around the nation. But the same general pattern of evolution could be seen from coast to coast.

The name "Sweet Auburn" became synonymous with wealth and status—*relative* wealth and status, to be sure, but impressive by any standard. Alonzo Herndon, who in 1906 had had the foresight to close his barbershop before the rampaging white mob arrived, went on to become Atlanta's first black millionaire. He founded the Atlanta Life Insurance Company, the biggest black-owned insurer in the nation, and put his physical stamp on Sweet Auburn with an opulent headquarters building and other projects. The Herndon family home, with towering white columns that make it look almost like a plantation manor— locals called it "Tara," Herndon called it "Old Glory"—was one of the most impressive residences in the city and a source of great pride for black Atlantans. The beaux arts mansion, painstakingly restored, is now a museum and research center dedicated to black Atlanta's rich history.

Herndon chose to build his home not in the Sweet Auburn neighborhood but to the west, near the other pole of black achievement in Atlanta—the University Center District. In 1950, 90 percent of black students pursuing postsecondary education were doing so at historically black colleges and universities. In other words, if you were young, gifted, and black, it was overwhelmingly likely that you would end up attending an all-black institution of higher learning—and quite likely that your dream would be to go to school in Atlanta.

For African Americans, Atlanta enjoyed the same status as a kind of latter-day Athens that Boston did for the larger society. There were elite black colleges and professional schools in other cities—Howard University in Washington, Fisk University and Meharry Medical College in Nashville. But nowhere else could there be found the critical mass that was assembled in Atlanta, where five abutting institutions offered not only a comprehensive range of undergraduate, graduate, and professional programs but also two unique campuses: Morehouse, an elite all-men's college, and Spelman, an elite all-women's college. Within black America, a degree from Morehouse or Spelman was the equivalent of a degree from Princeton or Wellesley. (Howard University reserved for itself the designation "the black Harvard," though generations of Morehouse men would disagree.)

Surrounding Sweet Auburn and the University Center District was a vibrant black community dedicated to upward mobility. The city's first black-owned office building, built by Henry Rucker in 1904, sheltered the dreams of generations of black entrepreneurs. The Royal Peacock (called the Top Hat Club when it was founded in 1938) became a regular venue for the country's top-flight black entertainers—much like the Lincoln Theatre and the Howard Theater in the U Street area, the heart of Washington's African American community, or the famed Apollo Theater on 125th Street in Harlem. Reporters from the black-owned *Atlanta Daily World* worked to provide black Atlanta's citizens with news they could use. Over the years, black visitors from out of town found lodgings at black-owned establishments like the Royal and Savoy hotels and the University Motel. Everyone ate at Paschal's Restaurant, famous for its fried chicken. Thriving black churches gave the community moral cohesion and performed many of the social services that city officials reserved for whites and their neighborhoods. Such was the milieu (midcentury Atlanta; Ebenezer Baptist Church; Morehouse College; regular customer at Paschal's) that nurtured the Reverend Martin Luther King Jr.

There were class divisions, based not just on relative wealth but also on skin color—a phenomenon graphically illustrated by the philosophical struggle between the dark-brown, rough-hewn, up-by-his-bootstraps Booker T. Washington, who spoke for the black masses on the farms and in the slums, and the chestnut-colored, aquiline-featured, Harvard-trained W. E. B. DuBois, who placed his hopes for the advancement of the race in the educated elite that he called the "Talented Tenth." Atlanta's black elite was disproportionately light-skinned, and to gain access to the better social circles it helped to be able to pass the "paper-bag test"—a simple relationship of hue and value. A premium was placed on what used to be called "good" hair, meaning hair that could be described as wavy rather than kinky. There was a measure of what has to be called discrimination against those with the most purely "African" coloration and features. There were women who set out to nab "light-skinned" boyfriends, and there were men whose idea of beauty eliminated anyone with darker skin, or a broader nose, than the glorious Lena Horne.

But if the professionals who lived in big houses, belonged to the right social clubs, and went to the right parties were tempted to think they were superior to other black Atlantans, the Jim Crow system was always there to bring them back to the real world. Doctors, lawyers, and professors may have clustered in the "better" black neighborhoods, but those were contiguous to middle-income or lower-income areas—and never very far from the slums. And no string of college degrees, however impressive, gave the bearer a pass to sit anywhere near the front of a municipal bus.

Black Atlanta was peopled by solid citizens like Ruby Blackburn. Born in 1901 in a small Georgia town, she attended Morris Brown College in Atlanta and the Apex Beauty School. She opened Ruby's Beauty Shop on the west side of Atlanta, and that provided her livelihood.

But Blackburn is remembered for her work on behalf of her fellow black Atlantans. She was the founder of To Improve Conditions, a social club dedicated to black uplift. She organized the Cultural League Training Center, an agency dedicated to bettering the skills, working conditions, and earning potential of domestic workers. And she was the motivating force behind the formation of the Georgia League of Negro Women Voters, which pushed tirelessly for the constitutional rights that white Atlantans were so determined to withhold. I mention Blackburn because she was emblematic of her time—energetic, entrepreneurial, dedicated to progress, and rooted in her community. She was determined not only that she and other successful African Americans would continue their inexorable rise but that the entire race, given a chance, could and would come along.

It's important not to lose sight of the larger context: Compared in the aggregate to white Atlanta, black Atlanta was poor, undereducated, and underemployed. The luxury and excellence of Sweet Auburn and the universities glittered against a backdrop of meager housing, inadequate health care, neglected schools—and, given the environment, all the social ills that poverty so efficiently nourishes.

But just look at those once-rising inner-city communities today.

Alonzo Herndon's mansion, once the jewel of a neighborhood meant to overlook the sylvan college campuses, is crowded by development and decay. Sweet Auburn, long since bisected by a freeway, looks utterly unremarkable to anyone not familiar with its storied history; once the height of African American status and achievement, it is no longer the height of anything. Historical markers and spotty efforts at preservation are little more than a wish. The University Central District remains as a shrinking island in a troubled sea: Spelman and Morehouse are still elite and viable institutions, though not as exclusive as they once were, while Clark is struggling to recall its former glory. Morris Brown has lost its accreditation. It is true that black Atlanta is enjoying a renaissance, but the action is taking place miles away in the suburbs, where successful African Americans have clumped together, and in other parts of the city that used to be reserved for whites only.

In Atlanta, one of the most vibrant and successful African American communities in the nation underwent a long, slow process of disintegration. The same process took place across the country—as one black America, to all appearances indivisible, became four.

3 PARTING OF THE WAYS

How did disintegration happen? It was the gradual, natural, and perhaps inevitable product of both triumph and tragedy.

To understand how the process evolved, the best place to start is with the opening of the deepest and most significant cleavage in black America, involving by far the largest groups: the gap between the Mainstream and the Abandoned. The history of this separation is written on U Street in Washington, D.C.

Washington's obsessive-compulsive system of naming streets—letters, numbers, quadrants—offers no clue as to what a given neighborhood might look or feel like. To anyone unfamiliar with the city, "U St. NW" is, at most, a rough geographical marker. To Washingtonians, however, this spoonful of alphabet soup is full of local flavor—and redolent of black American history. The story of U Street is the story both of triumph and of disintegration.

I moved to the Washington area at the end of 1979. A couple of years later, a dear family friend came to visit—a man who wasn't a blood relative but had been taken in by my grandparents, becoming like an older sibling to my mother; when I was christened, she had asked him to be my godfather. I was driving him through the city, and when we happened to cross U Street he was suddenly flooded with nostalgia. When he had visited Washington as a young man in the 1950s, U Street was *the place*. He remembered the Lincoln Theatre, where he had heard Duke Ellington and Count Basie. He recalled the shops, the restaurants, the elegance, the sophistication, the snap and bustle, the prosperity, the nonstop action. U Street, any proud (and perhaps slightly chauvinistic) black Washingtonian would have told you, was just like Atlanta's Sweet Auburn, but with class instead of, ahem, crass.

But as I drove through town with my godfather, the U Street before our eyes was a very different place.

The Lincoln Theatre wasn't a showcase for the geniuses of jazz; it was a derelict shell that gave no hint of former glory. There were no shops anymore except cheap dollar-store-type establishments that sold a lot of tube socks, underwear, and hair products; there was certainly no elegance or sophistication. Restaurants included Ben's Chili Bowl, a brave survivor from the late 1950s, and a bunch of takeout joints. Wig shops and beauty salons held on by their (fake) fingernails. There was plenty of snap and bustle, all right, but of a different kind: U Street and its environs had become one of the city's most notorious open-air illegal drug markets, offering mostly heroin but now, as the hyped-up '80s began to gather steam, quickly diversifying into cocaine. At certain hours of the day, the empty street would magically fill with spectral figures who materialized out of boarded-up buildings and weed-choked empty lots; immediately, cold-eyed young men arrived to sell little. packets of bliss. Police called it "feeding time." When afternoon gave way to evening, the commerce of prostitution settled in for the night. U Street was an exciting place full of opportunity and enterprise, all right, but in a sense that could give only pushers and pimps a sense of accomplishment and pride.

That was nearly thirty years ago. Today U Street is one of the liveliest, most desirable neighborhoods in town. Old landmarks—not just the Lincoln Theatre but also the Bohemian Caverns nightclub, where past performers included Billie Holiday, Miles Davis, Ella Fitzgerald, John Coltrane, Louis Armstrong, Dizzy Gillespie, and just about every other mid-century jazz artist you've ever heard of—are open again for the amusement of moneyed young patrons. There is more retail commerce up and down the street than ever—make that more *legal* retail commerce—with funky boutiques selling what passes for hip fashion in buttoned-down Washington. Where once there were empty lots and burned-out shells, new apartment buildings offer anyone with a million dollars the opportunity to live in spacious, spanking-new "lofts" that look almost like the real thing. There are cafés and wine bars; there are stores selling designer furniture. Around the intersection with Ninth Street, a lively row of restaurants draws patrons from around the city.

The temptation is to say that U Street is "back," but that wouldn't be accurate. Sixty years ago, or certainly thirty years ago, you would have been surprised to see a Caucasian soul within blocks of U Street. Today, roughly half of the people you see out and about on U Street at any given moment are white. The restaurant row along Ninth Street is noteworthy in that the proprietors of most of the thriving new eateries are black—but they also happen to be recent immigrants from Ethiopia.

It is not my godfather's U Street.

The trajectory of black Washington's most storied district traces the arc of black America in the late twentieth century—a parabola of success, failure, rebirth, and divergence.

By the early 1960s, U Street had already passed its heyday. Inner cities had fallen out of fashion; those who could afford to do so, both black and white, were moving away. The streetcar system that once had knitted the city together was gone, and those with means—and automobiles—had moved to what was once considered the periphery. The newspaper heiress Katharine Graham, who grew up blocks away from U Street in a mansion on the other, much whiter side of Meridian Hill Park, had decamped to Georgetown, a neighborhood that became synonymous with power and wealth; Jack and Jackie Kennedy lived there, as did Pamela Harriman, Ben Bradlee and Sally Quinn, and later Bob Woodward. Few residents of Georgetown today are aware that they are living in what had once been largely a working-class black neighborhood before a prewar wave of gentrification had made it *the* place to live in Washington. Years from now, I suppose, only historians will know that U Street was once one of black America's jewels.

The first blow to U Street was a positive development: African Americans suddenly had more choices. Washington was always something of a special case in terms of how segregation worked. Lying south of the Mason-Dixon Line, it was in essence a Southern town. But it was the site of the federal government, which gave the city a unique status as neither fish nor fowl—it wasn't as relatively laissez-faire as some Northern cities but neither was it as rigidly locked down as an Atlanta or a Birmingham. And when change came, it often came to Washington first because of its federal status. President Truman integrated government workplaces in 1948, which opened employment opportunities to blacks in the city's principal industry. Under President Eisenhower, first parks and other recreation facilities and then the public schools were integrated in 1954. By 1957, Washington had become the first large U.S. city with an African American majority.

As strictures in public accommodations and the schools fell away, so did the formal and informal rules that had segregated the city's neighborhoods. Black families who lived in close-in enclaves such as LeDroit Park, up the hill from U Street near Howard University, departed for parts of the city that once would not have welcomed them, especially the leafy neighborhoods at the city's far northern tip. Or else African Americans fled all the way to the suburbs—more to the Maryland side than to Virginia—where new ranch-style homes and split-levels offered all the modern conveniences. This was a time, remember, when there was nothing remotely pejorative about the concept of suburban sprawl. Rather, it was seen as progress. Except in Manhattan and arguably in Chicago, urban density had become the antithesis of the American dream.

Many of the African Americans who once patronized upscale retail stores along U Street had moved away, and those who remained had other options. Blacks in Washington had long been able to go downtown and shop at the reasonably priced department stores like Hecht and Lansburgh, and they were even welcome at the midrange department store Woodward and Lothrop. For many years, however, they were not invited to patronize upscale Garfinckel's, which was the jewel of the main F Street shopping corridor not far from the White

House. Mrs. Lucille Foster, a longtime black Washingtonian who grew up in Georgetown and subsequently lived for many years near U Street, recalls that when she saw a particular dress in the window at Garfinckel's that she wanted to buy—with her own money—the wealthy white matron for whom she worked as a cook had to go into the store and make the purchase. By the mid-'60s, though, the doors of Garfie's were open to all—as were most restaurants and other places of business.

The need for a blacks-only venue like the Lincoln Theatre had disappeared, now that establishments downtown such as the grand Warner Theatre and the venerable National Theatre were happy, or at least willing, to welcome African Americans. The Bohemian Caverns lost its ability to attract top-line performers when integrated clubs opened their doors, such as Blues Alley in Georgetown, which was established in 1965 and became the city's principal venue for jazz. Soon only the people who lived nearby had any reason to go to U Street. Those local residents—the ones who couldn't or wouldn't move out of the old neighborhood—tended to be less educated and affluent than those who took advantage of the new possibilities that racial integration offered.

The public schools serving the U Street area began to decline, not just because of a lack of attention and funding from the authorities—the ultimate authority over the District of Columbia in those days was Congress, and since the city had (and still has) no voting representation in the House of Representatives or the Senate, there was no one to hold accountable for how the city was being run—but also because the student population changed. The stable, middle-class, two-parent families that were most likely to prepare their children for school were leaving. Those students who remained were unlikely to get the kind of support at home that produces sustained academic achievement. As standards began to slip, more of the best and brightest students were pulled out; either they ended up in private or parochial schools, or their families moved to the suburbs and sent them to public schools where expectations were high, discipline was strict, and going on to college was considered inevitable, not impossible.

Thurlow Tibbs, a prominent African American art dealer who died in 1997, once recalled of the old days on U Street: "We are forced to deal with one another on every economic level. In my block we had school teachers, a mail man, a retired garbage man, and a registrar of Howard University."[1] But by the late 1960s, many if not most of the educated professionals had moved away. A community that once had been racially segregated but economically and socially integrated was well on its way to becoming segregated in all three senses—black, poor, isolated.

A vacuum was developing on U Street, and into it came a rush of undesirable pathology—poverty, teen pregnancy, single motherhood, drugs, crime, growing isolation from the mainstream. Which is not to say that those things did not previously exist. There is a sense in which the hollowing out of the middle class on U Street simply allowed everyone to see dysfunction that had been there all along. There were always poor people on U Street; there were always single mothers; there were always "ladies of the night" and "dope fiends" and drunks. It's true that more of this pathology arrived, but it's also true that out-migration of affluent, intact families and the demise of the neighborhood's economic underpinnings made it easier to see the pathology that was already present. And the phrase "growing isolation from the mainstream" can be misunderstood. U Street was always isolated from mainstream white society—that was the whole reason for U Street's existence. What happened was that some black Washingtonians were allowed to join the white mainstream. Those who failed to make the shift—those left behind—became increasingly isolated from mainstream values, mores, and aspirations.

That was the situation on the morning of April 4, 1968. By that evening, the U Street neighborhood—and the rest of black America—had changed forever.

* * *

Crowds began gathering spontaneously up and down U Street when the shocking, tragic, unbelievable yet all-too-believable news from Memphis began to circulate. Black America was never monolithic, but at certain rare moments it had recognized a single leader and made him the repository of our hopes and dreams, the symbol of our perseverance and pride, the avatar of our relentless, righteous aspiration for the justice that America had promised but cruelly withheld. The Reverend Martin Luther King Jr. had become such a leader, and now he was dead, assassinated by a sniper as he stepped onto a balcony at the Lorraine Motel. Even the first news reports included the detail that the suspect, who was still at large, was a white man.

Among those who came to the intersection of Fourteenth and U streets—the heart of what was left of the U Street business district, and the place where King's organization, the Southern Christian Leadership Conference (SCLC), had its local headquarters—was a young activist named Stokely Carmichael. Born in Trinidad, Carmichael had attended nearby

Howard University and was a former national chairman of the Student Nonviolent Coordinating Committee. According to an account written later by editors and reporters of *The Washington Post*, Carmichael led a group of his student followers into Peoples Drug Store, an outlet of a local chain, and demanded that the white manager close the store immediately out of respect for King's death. The manager, G. N. Simirtzakis, immediately complied, and the students moved on to tell the rest of the U Street area's stores to close down.

Carmichael spent the rest of the evening shuttering all the area's stores and trying to keep a lid on the crowd's rising emotions—at one point noticing a young man who was brandishing a gun and wresting the weapon away from him. He was only partly successful, however. Grief and anger turned into widespread looting.

From the *Washington Post* account:

Youths with television sets, electrical appliances, clothing, shoes, and other items began streaming past Carmichael at 14th and U. Slipping away, he ducked into the doorway of the SCLC office, stood for a moment, and then dashed across 14th Street to get in a waiting Mustang and speed away. It was 10:40 P.M. Carmichael knew his actions were being watched closely by federal authorities. He has since said he was determined to give them no cause to arrest him. Clearly, his decision to close the stores was an important factor in collecting the crowd. But he and his aides made strenuous efforts to check the mob when it grew unruly. He took his exit at the precise point of no return—as the memorial street demonstration exploded into riot.[2]

Similar scenes were being played out in more than thirty cities nationwide and scores of smaller towns. The King assassination was too much to bear. It was not just a murder but a taking—the theft of our leader, our future, our reason for continuing to hope that America was finally ready to accept us as true Americans. The paroxysm of violence that followed was deliberately destructive: They take from us, we take from them.

In the end, of course, we took from ourselves. The self-destructive nature of the 1968 riots was evident to all, even as the mayhem was unfolding. Everyone could see what came of such explosions—the scars were still fresh from the riots in Watts in 1965, and Detroit and Newark in 1967. For most of the century, the term "race riot" had referred to rampages by white mobs—Atlanta in 1906, Washington in 1919, Tulsa in 1921. Now it was black America's term to explode with inchoate, insensate, indiscriminate rage.

In Washington, the night of April 4 saw widespread looting in the blocks around Fourteenth and U. It wasn't until the afternoon of Friday, April 5, that the fires began. Scores of buildings were set ablaze, not just in the U Street corridor but also in Columbia Heights, stretching up Fourteenth Street to the north, and along H Street Northeast, another historic black business district across town. Crowds estimated at up to twenty thousand clashed with police; firefighters had a hard time getting into the war zones and a harder time getting back out, in the end watching helplessly as the many individual columns of smoke merged into a funereal pall. The city's black mayor-commissioner, Walter E. Washington, who exercised limited authority by leave of Congress, was helpless to end the anarchy; a curfew and a ban on the sale of firearms and alcohol had little effect, as the rioters had already smashed their way into the gun stores and the liquor stores and taken what they wanted.

Federal officials were alarmed. President Lyndon B. Johnson ordered the deployment of more than thirteen thousand federal and National Guard troops in an attempt to restore order—the biggest armed federal occupation of an American city since the aftermath of the Civil War. Marines with machine guns were sent to guard the Capitol, while soldiers from the Third Infantry ringed the White House. The military presence succeeded in containing the violence to U Street, Columbia Heights, and H Street—Washington's white neighborhoods and commercial districts were untouched, as was the city's core of monuments and federal offices—but rioting in the affected areas continued until April 8. It petered out, finally, as white-hot anger cooled, supplies of looted alcohol were exhausted, and new targets became scarce.

Twelve people were killed in Washington—a remarkably small number, given the scale and duration of the riot—and 1,097 were injured. Six thousand people were arrested. Much more shocking than the human toll, however, was the physical devastation of the cityscape: More than 1,200 buildings were burned, including 900 stores. The historic African American commercial districts had been destroyed. Even amid the charred, still-smoking ruins, civic boosters pledged that U Street, H Street, and Columbia Heights would be rebuilt. In terms of physical and commercial infrastructure, they were right—although it took forty years for the phoenix to rise. But if they meant that those neighborhoods would someday be what they once had been, that they would be centers of black American prosperity, the optimists were dead wrong. The neighborhoods burned in the riots were gone forever. They had been disintegrated.

* * *

Such nihilistic spasms of arson in urban black centers, beginning with Watts in 1965 and culminating with the riots of April 1968 in Washington, Baltimore, Boston, Kansas City, Chicago, Detroit, and other cities from coast to coast—which the writer James Baldwin had predicted in 1963 in *The Fire Next Time*—had the effect of thinning out black communities that once had been dense and full of life. In the 1960s, for example, nearly 125,000 people lived in the neighborhoods for which Chicago's Roosevelt Road—the focus of that city's 1968 riot—served as the major commercial strip. By 1990, fewer than 50,000 remained.[3]

Nationwide, thousands of stores, apartment houses, and other buildings were burned to the ground; many others were damaged but left standing and unoccupied. Only a relatively small percentage of buildings in any neighborhood were actually destroyed or ruined. But the fires left rips in the fabric of the affected areas, and these voids were like sinkholes that drained away vitality and promise. Housing prices in riot-torn neighborhoods fell sharply; families sold out so they could spirit their children to safer surroundings, while longtime landlords decided that the risks and headaches just weren't worth it. Into the vacuum came a new breed of slumlords, whose business model made no accommodation for frills such as maintenance or repairs. More town houses, storefronts, and apartments became abandoned, some finding new use as trick pads for prostitutes, shooting galleries for junkies, and temporary domiciles for homeless squatters. Often the only way to deal with such a nuisance was to tear the building down—leaving yet another hole, yet another spirit-draining void.

In an important sense, however, the riots were more symptom than disease. They came amid a larger historical context—the relocation and eventual hollowing-out of the American industrial base. By the mid-1960s, the jobs that had sustained urban working-class black communities had already begun to pick up and move away.

Detroit is perhaps the most vivid example. When my father was growing up in nearby Ann Arbor, the Big Three automakers were the economic lifeblood of the region and an abundant source of steady, good-paying jobs for African Americans—an escalator, in effect, that led directly to the middle class. A union job at a Ford, General Motors, or Chrysler plant meant the ability to own a home, the security of a comfortable retirement, and, most important, the promise of a better life for the next generation. The factories of Dearborn, Flint, and Pontiac were full of black men who might not have made it past high school but whose children damn well would. The dream that had inspired the Great Migration—a job, a home, a better life for the children—was coming true. But it didn't last.

Between 1948, when Detroit was enjoying an expansive postwar boom, and 1967, the year of the devastating Detroit riot, the city lost more than 130,000 manufacturing jobs.[4] Most of these were in the auto industry, which was already well advanced in the process of abandoning its storied birthplace. Building and retooling old factories in crowded, expensive Detroit no longer made sense, given the alternatives; the automakers had begun shifting their operations to new, more versatile and efficient plants built on former cow pastures in the rural Midwest and

South. Even the legendary Detroit-area plants, the ones so big they were worlds unto themselves—Dodge Main, with its thirty thousand workers, or Ford's gargantuan River Rouge complex, which employed ninety thousand at its height—had begun to shrink.

Similar transformations were taking place around the country. The steel mills left Pittsburgh, relieving the city of a noxious pall of smog but also taking away a reliable source of employment. The stockyards and slaughterhouses left Chicago, revealing a magnificent—but largely jobless—waterfront. (Washington was an exception; it didn't have any heavy industry to lose, and its main employer, the federal government, was recession-proof.) Of course, this wasn't just happening to black America; it was a wrenching adjustment for the whole nation, and the impact on working-class whites was profound. But blacks had been systematically kept at a disadvantage—they were generally the last hired, the first fired, and the least insulated against the cold new reality. Changes that were difficult for all working-class urban communities proved devastating for black America.

The combination of industrial transformation, devastation from the riots, and the advent of new options led many African Americans to move out of the inner cities. For years they had been streaming out of Washington to the northern and eastern reaches of the city and then beyond, establishing footholds in the suburbs. After the riots, the stream became a flood—especially to Prince George's County, Maryland, which in those days was mostly white and semirural, a land of pickup trucks and good old boys.

This movement would not have been possible before the passage of the Fair Housing Act of 1968, which prohibited

"discrimination in the sale, rental, and financing of dwell-
ings, and in other housing-related transactions, based on race,
color, national origin, religion, sex, familial status (including
children under the age of 18 living with parents or legal custo-
dians, pregnant women, and people securing custody of children under the age of 18), and handicap (disability)."[5] With
that legislation, restrictive housing covenants banning blacks
and other "undesirables" were invalidated—and black people,
for the first time, had the right to live in neighborhoods like
mine.

From today's vantage point, it is hard to imagine how per-
vasive these covenants were or what a big role they played in
keeping blacks (and often Jews) out of neighborhoods where
they were not wanted. Researching a planned remodeling of
my suburban house in 1997, I discovered that technically I
wasn't supposed to be living there—a longstanding covenant
constrained property owners to sell only to whites. These
restrictions are now patently illegal, of course, but once they
were valid contractual agreements and enforceable by law. As
far as I can tell, the whites-only covenant in my neighborhood
has never been formally erased, although the Fair Housing Act
made it not worth the paper it was written on.

It's wrong to think of the 1968 riots as the One Definitive
Moment when black America ceased to exist as a coherent
entity or to serve as a useful concept. The fragmentation of
America's once-whole black communities—a process which,
it is important to keep in mind, was greatly beneficial overall—had begun at least a decade earlier, and it took decades
longer to progress to the point of being fully recognizable. But
it is true that black America was different after the 1968 riots,
physically and psychologically.

Earlier that year, the report issued by the Kerner Commission on the 1967 Detroit and Newark riots had ventured a famously pessimistic assessment: "Our nation is moving toward two societies, one black, one white—separate and unequal."[6] In fact, those separate but unequal societies had existed for decades; perhaps the grandees of official Washington hadn't noticed that the lunch counters they patronized all those years were segregated, or maybe all of them were out of town when the March on Washington took place in 1963. But the riots came at a moment when things were changing, when walls were being demolished. White America was opening doors that once had been closed to black citizens. What the riots accomplished was to give some African Americans—those who were best prepared—a powerful incentive to walk through those newly opened doors and participate fully in the larger society.

No one quite realized it at the time, but black America was being split.

Some moved out—to neighborhoods unscarred by the riots, to the suburbs, to new developments in what once was farmland—and moved up, taking advantage of new opportunities. They moved up the ladder at work, purchased homes and built equity, sent their children to college, demanded and earned most of their rightful share of America's great bounty. They became the Mainstream majority.

Some didn't make it. They saw the row houses and apartment buildings where they lived begin to sag from neglect; they hunkered down as big public housing projects, conceived and built as instruments of "progress" and uplift, became increasingly dysfunctional and dangerous. They sent their children to low-performing schools that had already been forsaken by the brightest students and the pushiest parents. They remained while jobs left the neighborhood, as did capital, as did ambition, as did public order. They became the Abandoned.

* * *

The year 1967 saw the beginning of another form of divergence in black America. On June 12 of that year, the Supreme Court issued a unanimous decision written by Chief Justice Earl Warren. In the second paragraph of his opinion, Warren set out the facts of the case:

> In June 1958, two residents of Virginia, Mildred Jeter, a Negro woman, and Richard Loving, a white man, were married in the District of Columbia pursuant to its laws. Shortly after their marriage, the Lovings returned to Virginia and established their marital abode in Caroline County. At the October Term, 1958, of the Circuit Court of Caroline County, a grand jury issued an indictment charging the Lovings with violating Virginia's ban on interracial marriages. On January 6, 1959, the Lovings pleaded guilty to the charge and were sentenced to one year in jail; however, the trial judge suspended the sentence for a period of 25 years on the condition that the Lovings leave the State and not return to Virginia together for 25 years. He stated in an opinion that: "Almighty God created the races white, black, yellow, malay and red, and he placed them on separate continents. And but for the interference with his arrangement there would be no cause for such marriages. The fact that he separated the races shows that he did not intend for the races to mix."[7]

Richard and Mildred Loving had violated several Virginia laws, among them a statute that said: "If any white person intermarry with a colored person, or any colored person intermarry with a white person, he shall be guilty of a felony and shall be punished by confinement in the penitentiary for not less than one nor more than five years."[8]

The Lovings left Virginia to make their home in the District of Columbia. But in 1963, while U Street was beginning to hollow out and African Americans invaded the Maryland suburbs, the Lovings filed a court motion to vacate their felony sentences on grounds that the laws under which they were convicted were unconstitutional. In *Loving v. Virginia*, the Supreme Court ruled emphatically that no state had the right to restrict a citizen's right to marry on the basis of race. Laws banning interracial marriage in seventeen states were invalidated. The practice that Southerners referred to as "miscegenation" was now legally protected by the Constitution.

Of course, liaisons between whites and blacks had been common—if unacknowledged—since slavery began. Studies of genetic markers indicate that roughly 20 percent of African Americans' genes are of European origin[9]; the wide range of skin-color variation, not just among the black American population but within families, testifies to a long history of interracial congress. Primarily this consisted of forced or coerced sexual relations between white slave owners and black slaves. My wife, Avis, is a collector of African American historical artifacts and documents, and one of the items she found is a handbill announcing a slave auction in Charleston in 1833. Several of the women being sold are described as "likely"—not in the modern sense of "probable" but the archaic sense of "good-looking." Perhaps that is what Thomas Jefferson saw in his slave Sally Hemings, whose children, it is now generally agreed, Jefferson fathered.

In some other slave-owning countries, the mulatto off-spring of such unions were recognized as a distinct intermediate racial class. In the United States, however, mulatto meant black. The mixed-race, lighter-skinned progeny of slave owners sometimes were assigned to work as house slaves rather than field slaves, but they were still slaves. Since house duties required a certain amount of education and acculturation, many of those best prepared to lead and prosper after emancipation were light-skinned; if you look at photographs of the most prominent black citizens of Atlanta during Reconstruction, for example, you see that they're not actually very black. But Jim Crow put an end to any notion that blacks with obvious European ancestry were somehow "better" than blacks with no evident European genes. One drop of African blood was all it took to be consigned to the "colored" water fountain and the back of the bus.

The Jim Crow–era taboo against interracial relationships was never absolute—that would have been impossible—but it was powerful, even in the North. The proscription against mixed marriage, which conferred society's official blessing, was stronger, even in states where it was not punishable by years in prison. There had been famous exceptions—the heavyweight boxing champion Jack Johnson scandalized the nation in the early years of the twentieth century by openly cavorting with a succession of white women. But until the late 1950s or early '60s—around the time when the Lovings fell in love—the plot of *Guess Who's Coming to Dinner* would have qualified as science fiction.

The multiple social revolutions of the 1960s changed all

that. One early result was a baby boy named Barack Obama—born August 4, 1961, the son of a dashing Kenyan academic and a young white woman from Kansas, who, like so many of her peers, was opening her eyes to a dazzling array of new possibilities. By the end of the decade, American society's views on race and sexuality were radically changed. Interracial relationships were not yet commonplace, but they had lost all power to shock. In a reversal of the historic pattern, a majority involved black men and white women. These unions, inevitably, produced issue: a growing number of biracial children. Like Obama, most came to self-identify as African American—the as-yet-unrepealed one-drop rule that applies in our society, categorizing anyone partly black as fully black, gives them no real choice in the matter. But their relationship with white America is necessarily different from, say, mine. I can harbor a kind of residual bitterness that would not be possible if one of my parents were white.

It is hard to pin down a number of black-white biracial Americans; the latest census figures count 6.8 million citizens who self-classify as multiracial,[10] but this includes any possible combination in the whole "American Indian or Alaska Native; Asian; Black or African American; Native Hawaiian or Other Pacific Islander; and White" Census Bureau matrix—and also misses biracial men and women, such as President Obama, whose identification as African American is so strong that they simply classify themselves as "black." But it is clear that this segment—one of two groups forming a new black American that I call the Emergent—is growing. It owes its increase not just to love but also to the Lovings.

* * *

If we fast-forward to the present day, return to U Street and walk to the intersection of Ninth, we can see—and hear—the other key Emergent group. The street sounds suddenly change. You overtake a group of men having an animated discussion, and you notice that the conversation isn't in English, it's in Amharic. You walk past a record store, and the music you hear isn't hip-hop, it's Ethiopian pop. You take a whiff outside one of the neighborhood's busy restaurants and the smells are of *berbere, korerima*, and *mitmita*, spices used to prepare an exotic and ancient—but no less soulful—variety of soul food. Ninth and U is a focal point of Washington's Ethiopian and Eritrean immigrant community, the biggest in the nation.

Roughly one of every ten black people living in the Washington metropolitan area is foreign-born.[11] Ethiopians are the largest and most visible group, but the immigrants include Nigerians, Jamaicans, Liberians, Haitians—foot soldiers in the biggest influx of black people from Africa and the Caribbean since the importation of slaves was outlawed in 1807. These Emergent newcomers are making waves—in black America and beyond—far more impressive than their swelling numbers.

The impact is quiet and largely unheralded, but it is enormous. Africans are the best-educated group of immigrants coming to live in the United States—not Asians from China or India, not Europeans from Britain or France, not Latin Americans from Brazil or Argentina, but Africans from Nigeria, Ghana, South Africa, Senegal, Côte d'Ivoire. We don't notice because African immigrants, following the traditional pattern, often have to start at the bottom, working at jobs that take advantage of only a fraction of these newcomers' intelligence, experience, and ability.

A potent illustration of this came to me at the office. At *The Washington Post*, where I work, executives understandably became much more concerned about security after the September 11 terrorist attacks. New procedures were instituted, new radio-chip ID cards were issued, new rules were imposed limiting access to the alleys that ran along two sides of the building. The security guards, who worked for a contractor hired by the paper, were moved around according to some theory of how best to intercept and thwart a terrorist attack. One day, as I was navigating the new security gauntlet, I asked one of the guards—Mr. Massey, a middle-aged gentleman from Nigeria—whether any of this was making me safer. "Not at all," he said, and then he proceeded to explain that the new barriers and guard posts had been put in places where they would do nobody any good. Mr. Massey pointed out the weaknesses that were not being addressed and the potential entrances not being patrolled or even monitored by cameras. I asked how he came to speak so authoritatively, and he explained that before coming to this country he had retired from a long career in the Nigerian military. He'd learned about defensive emplacements during a period of study at Sandhurst, the British military academy. Prince Charles had also been studying at Sandhurst at the time. Mr. Massey had tried to explain this to his bosses at the security firm, but they blew him off. "I'm just a Nigerian," he said.

Ethiopian restaurateurs, Nigerian military officers, and most of the rest of today's African and Caribbean immigrants wouldn't be here if not for a series of laws beginning, coincidentally, about the same time that America began its process of disintegration. Immigrants from the Caribbean began to arrive in larger numbers after passage of the Hart-Cellar Act of 1965.

The law loosened restrictions on immigration based on geography—a system that favored Europeans over nonwhites—and shifted the emphasis to professional qualifications and family reunification. Subsequent measures in 1976 and 1980 made it easier for immigrants to come to the United States as students or refugees; an attempt at comprehensive immigration reform in 1986 allowed many undocumented immigrants to apply for legal status, including 135,000 from the Caribbean and Africa. For Africans, the key impetus was passage of the Immigration Act of 1990, which increased the number of immigrants admitted on the basis of their skills. The 1990 legislation also established a lottery system offering "diversity" visas to citizens of countries that were underrepresented in the immigrant population. The lottery was conceived—at a time when Latin Americans were arriving in droves—as a way to admit more Europeans who might not have relatives here to sponsor them. In other words, it was supposed to be a back door for more white folks to slip in. No one anticipated that the measure would open a major new pipeline for Africans, but it did: Between 1986 and 2006, more than one-quarter of all the available diversity visas went to sub-Saharan Africans.[12]

Many African-born doctors, lawyers, engineers, and other professionals are working quietly and unnoticed as nurses, paralegals, draftsmen—and security guards. In Washington, Ethiopian immigrants have found a viable niche in the parking industry as garage attendants and cashiers. Drivers of the city's huge fleet of taxicabs are as diverse and polyglot as the United Nations, but Africans form a major and perhaps dominant bloc. African immigrants aren't making waves—but their children are a different story.

Right now, the immigrant community is best described

as Emergent. In ten years, more expansive language may be required.

* * *

In 1939, a tract of land in Washington's northeast quadrant, near the Anacostia River, was transformed into the Langston Golf Course. It is the scruffiest of the city's three public courses, the toughest to play, and in many ways it's my favorite because of its history: Langston was established as a segregated facility. It was where black golfers, and only black golfers, were allowed to play. On any given Saturday, in the years before integration, out on the course you would have found doctors and lawyers, black celebrities who happened to be in town, and a few guys with swings so sweet that they might have been able to make a living on the professional tour, if blacks had been allowed. Lee Elder, one of the first African Americans who did get to play on the pro tour, managed the Langston course for a time after he retired from competition.

Things are different now. As I write this paragraph, I'm also watching a golf tournament on television. I ought to turn it off but I won't, and the reason is simple: Tiger Woods is moving up the leaderboard. On the last hole, he made an impossible birdie putt from the fringe. Now, from a hundred yards, he's just hit a wedge to within inches of the pin. It looks as if a Transcendent moment may be coming, and I don't want to miss it.

Woods is part of the last of the four black Americas—the Transcendent elite that has climbed to the absolute pinnacle of American society. There have always been African Americans who had power, influence, or wealth, but they were a comparative elite, rich and powerful within the context of black

American society. The new Transcendent black elite is rich and powerful within any context, by any conceivable standard. Forty years ago, which would have seemed more likely: that a black man would be elected president of the United States, or that a black man would become absolute lord and master of golf—*golf!*—a pastime redolent of wealth, influence, and long afternoons at the whites-only country club.

For that matter, what were the odds that a black woman, born into poverty in rural Mississippi, would become a billionaire who wields immense power, not just in television but in book and magazine publishing, theater, philanthropy, and apparently whatever new world she decides to conquer? That a black man from Philadelphia who began his entertainment career as a rapper would become the biggest movie star in Hollywood? That a black woman from Birmingham, a childhood friend of one of the four girls killed in the 1963 terrorist bombing at the Sixteenth Street Baptist Church, would chart the nation's foreign policy as secretary of state?

The temptation is to just keep running down the Transcendent roster—Venus and Serena Williams, Queen Latifah, Chris Rock—but you get the point. The nation is long accustomed to African American preeminence in entertainment and sports. But now there's also the billionaire Robert L. Johnson, who founded Black Entertainment Television. There's also the growing number of performer-tycoons, such as Sean "P. Diddy" Combs and Shawn "Jay-Z" Carter, who have expanded beyond the music business to create their own mini-conglomerates— fashion, fragrances, television, whatever—and now take the stage only as a means of burnishing the brand.

How it happened that a small but growing group of African Americans reached the top is no mystery. All it took was opportunity—created by the civil rights revolution—and time. Forty years ago, remember, only 2 percent of African Americans had incomes of $100,000 or more.[13] Now more than 10 percent earn at least that much—and a small but growing number of black Americans earn many times more.

The Transcendents have impact far beyond their numbers. Someday America will get used to seeing African Americans in positions of supreme authority, wealth, or influence—exhibiting all the patterns of behavior that such status implies. When that day comes, Skip Gates won't have to worry about being arrested in his own home for being insufficiently deferential to a white cop. We're not quite there yet.

* * *

It took forty years. At times the process was gradual, at times abrupt, at times even violent. In the end, one black America became four—Mainstream, Abandoned, Transcendent, and Emergent. And the way to understand the African American condition today is first to examine all four.

4 THE MAINSTREAM: A DOUBLE LIFE

We live in two worlds. That may be the most overused cliché about the black Mainstream, but it's also a central reality for most African Americans of my generation—working in integrated settings where we are often unsure of where we stand, socializing in black settings where solidarity flows from shared history and experience. A close second, cliché-wise, would be to point out that Sunday morning is the most segregated time of the week in America, when blacks and whites attend their separate churches.

But these statements of the obvious help make a more subtle point: A great deal of Mainstream black life is lived exclusively, or almost exclusively, among black people. Some would call this self-segregation. The pull of racial affinity remains strong among baby boomers, but our children, the millennials, don't feel it the way we do. In the long term, that's good for the nation; for now, it leads to friction within families and a generational divide.

Begin with the basic question of where to live. Mine was the first cohort of Mainstream black Americans who reached adulthood with the legal right and the financial resources to settle anywhere we wanted. Since we had been born into a world when African Americans had fewer options, our choices were partly pragmatic and partly political. Some, like our family, decided to integrate what had been all-white or mostly white neighborhoods. Many others decided to make a different statement.

In the Washington area, where I have watched this process unfold over the past three decades, more African Americans now live in the suburbs than in the District of Columbia itself. While there is a significant black presence in all the surrounding counties, the size of that presence varies greatly. The Potomac River is a powerful dividing line—far more African Americans live to the east and north of the river, in the Maryland suburbs, than in the Virginia suburbs to the west and south.

There are plenty of reasons why this overall pattern might arise. When the Mainstream exodus began, neighborhoods in the western part of the city were mostly white and those in the eastern part mostly black; the Maryland suburbs were closer and more familiar for African Americans who were ready to move. And while both states are south of the Mason-Dixon Line, Virginia means "Dixie" in a way that Maryland doesn't. Still, proximity and "Dixieness" don't explain why the Potomac is such a sociological barrier. We're talking about a compact metropolitan area where distance shouldn't be much of a factor one way or the other; rush-hour traffic is equally hellacious no matter what starting point you choose on the circumferential Beltway. The close-in Virginia suburbs are politically liberal, and while there was a time when they wouldn't have accepted large numbers of black newcomers, that hasn't been an issue at least since I moved to the area, which was three decades ago. Back then, jurisdictions like Arlington or Alexandria in Virginia were smart, tolerant, progressive bastions compared to Maryland's Prince George's County, which was mostly white and semirural, full of good old boys who drove pickup trucks and women who sported some of the last non-ironic beehives in America.

Yet today, Arlington has a black population of less than 10 percent. Prince George's, where two-thirds of the residents are African American, is the most affluent black-majority county in the nation, with a median household income of about $68,000 a year.

The second-richest is DeKalb County, just east of Atlanta, with a median household income of about $52,000. In both cases, these averages are a distortion in the same way that the median household income figure for Manhattan—$63,704, as of 2007—doesn't tell you about the heiresses and trophy wives who spend that much on clothes and personal grooming every month. Prince George's and DeKalb aren't Manhattan, but in parts of both counties six-figure incomes are the norm.

In Prince George's, an unincorporated town called Mitchellville is the place to begin any examination of the upwardly mobile black Mainstream. Nearly 80 percent of Mitchellville's 10,000 residents are African American. The mean household income in 2007 was $104,786—compared to $68,080 for the state of Maryland as a whole—and the average home cost a bit more than $500,000.[1] Many of the houses are "Mitchellville Mansions"—cavernous, newly built structures with soaring entryways, multicar garages, and a design sensibility that could be called random historical nouveau: here a Palladian window, there a set of Doric columns, everywhere a joyous mash-up of architectural time and space. A dwelling of six thousand square feet would be considered fairly modest.

Mitchellville's unofficial boundaries encompass Woodmore, a gated community built around a country club and golf course. Just to the south is Lake Arbor, another exclusive community surrounding a golf course. Not far away is a golf course called Lake Presidential. The University of Maryland's main campus is in Prince George's, and the school's golf course is open to the public. More than a dozen other public and private courses make Prince George's County an epicenter of African American golf. On any reasonably clement spring, summer, or fall afternoon, you could tee off anywhere in the county and it would be perfectly normal to see an all-black foursome ahead of you and another one behind. They might be lawyers, doctors, government contractors, retired military; they might be ambitious professional women trying to learn the secret winks and nods of the executive suites. They might be beginners, but they also might be extremely good. Quiet as it was kept, African Americans were playing golf long before Tiger Woods was born.

The critical mass of black achievement and prosperity in Prince George's didn't just happen. The county was a logical destination for middle-class black families who were ready to abandon the city—it was the least-developed close-in county with the most-affordable land. But there was no compelling reason for those Mainstream families to clump together other than preference. Many later arrivals settled in Prince George's not because that was where they could buy the biggest and best house for the least money but because they wanted to participate in the project of creating a black community like none other in the nation.

To be part of this upper-Mainstream enclave, they were willing to make compromises and sacrifices. The Prince George's schools are better than those in the District of Columbia (which isn't saying much) but not nearly as highly regarded as those in other Washington suburbs. Parts of the county, particularly those near the D.C. line, are suffering "spillover dysfunction" as gentrification pushes poor people out of the city proper; towns like Capitol Heights are plagued by drug dealing and crime. County government has seen an embarrassing series of corruption scandals, and the county police force has a reputation for shooting first and asking questions later, if at all. Top-of-the-line retailers like Nordstrom, Saks Fifth Avenue, and Neiman Marcus have bypassed the county in favor of other Washington-area jurisdictions with similar income figures, as have celebrity-chef restaurants and other luxury-class amenities. Prince George's residents often complain of being overlooked and undervalued, and they often suspect that these slights are not a matter of economics but of race.

And that is one important regard in which the Mainstream black experience differs from that of other middle-class Americans: Despite all the progress that's been made, there's still a nagging sense of being looked down upon, of being judged, of being disrespected. What keeps this difference alive is that these suspicions aren't always paranoia. They're not always justified, either, but there's enough reality behind them to keep alive a sense of separate but not-quite equal—enough to make many people seek safety, acceptance, and solidarity in numbers.

* * *

Prince George's is home to distinguished black scholars, professionals, athletes, and other pillars of respectable society. It is also home to the best-selling author who writes under the pseudonym Zane. This is not to suggest that there is anything untoward or dishonorable about Zane's success—she's one of the most prolific and popular African American writers working today—but simply to note that it's not the kind of achievement often celebrated in church or the classroom. Her niche is steamy, explicit, erotic fiction aimed at black female readers, and books such as *Addicted, The Sex Chronicles: Shattering the Myth*, and *The Sex Chronicles 2: Gettin' Buck Wild* have made her a star in the publishing world. Think of her work as romance fiction in which the characters are black, anatomically correct, conscious of their sexual needs, and both diligent and imaginative at fulfilling them. Euphemisms like "throbbing manhood" are replaced by simpler, less ambiguous terms.

I mention Zane not so much because of her books but because of her readers. Much has been written about the decline of the two-parent household among African Americans. The focus has been mostly on the Abandoned—young single mothers, babies having babies. But this trend is also a Mainstream phenomenon. Yale University researchers have found that highly educated black women are especially likely to be unmarried and independent, and that they are increasingly unlikely to find black husbands of comparable accomplishment—black women pursuing postgraduate studies outnumber black men by almost two to one. Potential husbands come in other colors, of course, but studies show that black women, at least to this point, have been much less open to the possibilities of interracial marriage than black men.

In other words, in places like Prince George's and DeKalb there is a substantial population of successful, independent black women who have never been married and never will be. Add them to the black women who are separated or divorced, and you've identified a large and growing segment of Mainstream black America. There is, so far, no truly analogous group among whites or other minorities; numbers of female SALAs (single adults living alone) are increasing throughout society, but nowhere has the rise been nearly as rapid or as significant as among African Americans. According to the Census Bureau, 21 percent of adult white women have never been married. Among adult black women, the figure is a stunning 42 percent.[2]

These unattached women are giving a new twist to an old and disputed idea, which is that black America is essentially a matriarchy. The meta-narrative goes something like this: From the earliest days of slavery, black men were prized and of course exploited, but also feared and envied. In the imagination of white society, black men were imputed to have superhuman strength and sexual prowess, which was threatening to white men at the most primal level. Black men were thus subjected to the most sadistic tortures. After emancipation, the black man still had to be kept down; when the uppity black fighter Jack Johnson—who had the audacity to date white women publicly—defeated the white former heavyweight champion Jim Jeffries on July 4, 1910, in what had been billed as the "Fight of the Century," angry whites rioted in cities across the nation.

The black woman, though, was less of a threat. Given more space in American society, she became the mainstay of the black family—she kept a steady job, she went to church, she supported her man when the world was too much for him to bear, she forgave him when he strayed, she provided stability and continuity, she raised the children, she subjugated her own needs to those of her man and her family. She was the rock, the anchor, the queen.

But what is an anchor without a ship? To me, this is one of the most interesting developments in the evolution of Mainstream black America: Millions of women are on their own, improvising their way through life. Just in my circle of friends, I know single black women who have decided to have children but not get married, adopt children on their own, or take in the children of relatives who, for whatever reason, are unable to care for them. I also know black women who don't want children but wouldn't mind a husband. I know black women who use their disposable income to travel constantly and in great style, with Paris being a popular destination; Josephine Baker was a powerful role model.

Almost every accomplished, Mainstream, single black woman I know is involved in some kind of volunteer project whose aim is to uplift the Abandoned—reading to schoolchildren, mentoring teenage girls, helping victims of domestic violence. Almost every one belongs to at least one book club. Almost all date black men, when a suitable black man presents himself, but almost none date white men. None seems "desperate to find a man," and most seem quite happy—with good jobs, high incomes, and no children or spouse to worry about, they tend to be financially savvy and secure. Most own their homes. Almost all the single black women of my acquaintance go to church regularly, but few see any contradiction between spending the morning in a pew singing hymns and the evening curled up with one of Zane's X-rated tomes.

The uncertain marriage prospects of educated, single black women are usually presented as some sort of tragedy, but that's not the impression I get. I see instead a fascinating process of self-invention, and I think I might be seeing American society's most radical experiment in rewriting the definitions of household, family, and fulfillment.

The truth is that I never fully bought the matriarchy idea. But I always thought that the women's movement was mostly old news to African American women. They were long accustomed to juggling family and career, well acquainted with the tradeoffs that modern life demands. Now, I believe, Mainstream black women may be blazing another trail that the rest of American society will follow as we redefine the concepts of household and family. In this sense, the black Mainstream is at the cutting edge of societal evolution.

* * *

It is hard to overstate how heroic the Mainstream's rise has been. Larger numbers of African Americans have made a greater advance, and done so more swiftly, than has been the case with any other significant "outsider" group that successfully pushed, charmed, or clawed its way into the American middle class. Just as it's wrong to ignore the overlapping pathologies of poverty, hopelessness, unemployment, crime, incarceration, and family disintegration that plague black Americans disproportionately, it's also wrong to deny that the rise of the black Mainstream is truly a great American success story—arguably, the greatest of all.

To state the obvious, African American progress cannot be measured from the very beginning—the arrival of the first African slaves at Jamestown in 1619. (The Spanish had brought some Africans to Florida decades earlier, but that turned out to be a false start.) For more than half the elapsed time since, black progress was not just discouraged, not just hampered, but actually outlawed—in South Carolina, Georgia, and other Southern states, it was against the law to teach a slave to write. These restrictions against black literacy—in effect, laws to prevent black intellectual development, which was rightly considered dangerous—became more draconian, not less so, during slavery's final tumultuous decades. White Southerners had long lived in constant fear of black insurrection, and in 1831 the Nat Turner revolt in Southampton County, Virginia, turned that fear into something like sheer panic throughout the slave-owning states. In Mississippi, for example, legislators promptly passed a new law requiring all free blacks to leave the state, lest they incite the slaves by educating them.

It is equally useless to take emancipation as a starting point. This is not just because of the enormous deficits that newly freed blacks faced. Without assets or education they had to start from scratch, but during Reconstruction they made rapid gains. The problem was that those gains were promptly and often brutally taken away by Southern officials when Reconstruction was abruptly halted. This betrayal was committed with the acquiescence of the federal government—which was more interested in reaching an accommodation with the South than in following through on General Sherman's promise of "forty acres and a mule"—and a stunningly racist Supreme Court. Jim Crow laws in the South deliberately kept the building blocks of meaningful development—education, opportunity, wealth that could be passed down through the generations—out of African American hands. Black advancement simply wasn't allowed.

This situation, in which African Americans were deliberately and at times brutally held down, persisted through the first two-thirds of the twentieth century. In 1945, black sociologists St. Clair Drake and Horace R. Cayton published *Black Metropolis*, a landmark study of the huge African American community in Chicago. Benefiting from extensive data collected during the Depression by WPA researchers, the book is perhaps the most comprehensive and vivid portrait ever assembled of separate but unequal black America. The authors devote one chapter to "The Job Ceiling"—the strictures that confined most blacks to semiskilled, unskilled, or "servant" jobs where the pay was low and the opportunity for advancement, for "betterment of the race," was close to nil. In 1940, according to Drake and Cayton, nearly 75 percent of employed black men in Chicago and more than 85 percent of employed black women worked in these low-paid categories as gardeners, housemaids, janitors—menial jobs, essentially, that entailed providing services to whites.[3]

For black men, even those with a better-than-average education, there was security rather than shame in working as a Pullman porter or a Red Cap luggage handler—two occupations so dominated by African Americans that they were known in the community as "Negro jobs." Chicago was by far the nation's busiest and most vital railway hub, and trains were vastly more important as a means of long-distance travel than they are today. In 1930, of the approximately nine thousand Pullman porters in the nation, about four thousand lived in Chicago and the great majority were black. Some in the African American community saw this hegemony in railroad service jobs as unfortunate. "We do not believe we should have a monopoly on Pullman porter service any more than that white people should have a monopoly on Pullman conductor service, or that Irishmen should have a monopoly on police and fire departments," the *Chicago Defender*, a leading black weekly, editorialized. But the pay was better than blacks could dream of in most other jobs, especially after the Brotherhood of Sleeping Car Porters, under the leadership of the legendary A. Philip Randolph, negotiated a contract that gave porters a "living wage." The additional cash that porters earned in tips elevated the job from tolerable to desirable.

Of the estimated six hundred Red Cap baggage handlers in Chicago, four hundred were African American. The black Red Caps were, generally, much better educated than their white colleagues; one union official reported that of the ninety African Americans in his local, seventy-two had at least some college and two were practicing physicians, according to Drake and Cayton.[4] For white men, hauling valises, suitcases, hatboxes, and steamer trunks through train stations was a low-status job. For black men, it was simply a job that offered mediocre pay but good tips, and thus could support a family. Status wasn't the point.

For black women, the default job was domestic service. The pay was low—during the Depression, the going rates were $2 a day for occasional work, $20 a week for steady employment—and conditions varied widely. Employers could be capricious, unreasonable, or abusive; their homes and habits could be filthy. Those were the "hard people to work for." Or a black domestic worker could be lucky enough to be employed by families that were consistent, thoughtful, and generous—

"nice people to work for." The families of women who worked for the "nice" folks could benefit from the employers' largess toward loyal retainers, which sometimes, though not usually, could be genuinely large; Mrs. Lucille Foster of Washington, for example, was given a new car every few years and ultimately even a house by the wealthy Georgetown family for whom she worked for decades, and the family went so far as to establish a trust to care for her in her old age. But this kind of generosity was rare. The more common and significant benefit that domestic workers received was the socialization that resulted from close daily contact with people who lived on a different plane of existence. They learned the white world with an intimacy that could only come from literally examining people's dirty laundry. This knowledge helped the workers and their families survive.

But these urban, sophisticated black men and women were stuck at the bottom of the income scale—and this was true even in Chicago, the boomtown with the big shoulders. Back in the South, millions of African Americans who hadn't joined the Great Migration were still tied to the land, not as slaves but as sharecroppers, tenant farmers, or hired labor. Official policy in the South was to keep blacks uneducated and dependent on white landowners for employment or subsistence. It is not possible to rise when you have a boot on your neck.

Progress has to be measured, then, roughly from the middle of the twentieth century, which is when the economic and social ambitions of African Americans began to change as new possibilities emerged. The first big impetus was World War II. The rapid mobilization of what was to become the world's biggest military-industrial complex provided instant employment, both voluntary and involuntary, for large numbers of African Americans, many of whom had been out of a job. In 1940, as war raged in Europe and U.S. industry geared up, A. Philip Randolph threatened a march on Washington to demand that African Americans be given some of the new jobs being created. President Franklin D. Roosevelt responded by creating a new federal committee to investigate and eliminate workplace discrimination. In the end, it didn't matter that Roosevelt's Fair Employment Practices Committee had no real power, thanks to the intervention of powerful Southern congressmen. There was simply no way to meet the wartime industrial demand without African American workers, who ended up with high-paying jobs they couldn't have dreamed of a few years earlier.

Once the United States entered the war, eligible black men volunteered or were drafted to serve in the military. Those who served in the segregated armed forces during the war years returned to civilian life with new skills, a new appreciation for their own potential, and a new attitude of entitlement and impatience. The old separate but unequal devil's bargain, which many blacks had long accepted—and which they had found ways to rationalize, since there appeared to be no way to change it—was no longer tolerable.

Those stirrings of militancy helped produce the second big push: the civil rights movement. That great, tumultuous struggle culminated in 1964 and 1965 when President Lyndon B. Johnson secured passage of the landmark Civil Rights Act and Voting Rights Act. Even then, however, black Americans had to struggle to force the nation to begin to fulfill the promises it had made more than a century earlier.

It's only possible to measure black progress from roughly forty years ago, when opportunity became more than a rumor.

And if you look at aggregate indices, you could argue that African Americans haven't come very far at all. In 2005, according to the Census Bureau, the median household income was $50,784 for non-Hispanic whites and $30,858 for blacks. That ratio—with black households earning about three-fifths of what white households earn—is about the same as it was in 1967, when the median household income was $36,895 for whites and $21,422 for blacks (in constant dollars).[5] To put it mildly, that's discouraging. It looks at first glance as if forty years of antidiscrimination laws, affirmative action programs, and relentless consciousness-raising have made African Americans wealthier as the whole society became wealthier—but that in relative terms, all this has gotten us precisely nowhere.

Look more closely, however, and the numbers tell two stories—one about the surging advance of the Mainstream, the other about the bitter retreat of the Abandoned.

In 1967, just 25.8 percent of black households had a median income of more than $35,000 in today's dollars; by 2005, however, 45.3 percent of black households had crossed that threshold. In those four decades, the percentage of black households earning more than $75,000 went from 3.4 to 15.7.[6] To be sure, much higher percentages of white households are affluent. But in terms of actual numbers, that meant roughly six million African Americans had become wealthy enough to live in spacious homes, buy luxury goods, travel abroad on vacation, spoil their children—to live, in other words, just like well-to-do white folks.

Those income figures are more impressive when you take geography into account. The Great Migration notwithstanding, a majority of African Americans have always lived in the South—where the cost of living is well below the national average. In recent years, a trend of reverse migration has seen increasing numbers of blacks moving south, not just to metropolitan centers like Atlanta or Charlotte but to smaller cities and towns as well. In Manhattan, living on $75,000 a year sounds like bare subsistence. In Jackson, Mississippi; Dothan, Alabama; or Kingstree, South Carolina, it sounds like a ticket to the promised land.

In education, given the centuries-long policy of keeping black people ignorant and unlettered, African American gains have been even greater. In 1967, 53.4 percent of whites but only 29.5 percent of blacks had completed high school, according to the Census Bureau. In 2008, the figures were 87.1 percent for whites and 83 percent for blacks—for all intents and purposes, full parity. In 1967, 10.6 percent of whites and only 4 percent of blacks had completed four years of college. In 2008, 29.8 percent of whites and 19.6 percent of blacks were college-educated—a threefold increase for whites but a quintupling for African Americans.[7] The oft-quoted "statistic" about there being more young black men in prison than in college—Barack Obama cited it during the presidential campaign—is wrong by miles; there are about three times as many college-age African American men on campus as there are behind bars. It's true that one big hurdle remains: While the percentage of African Americans entering college is approaching that of whites, significantly fewer black students stay long enough to graduate. But leaving college short of a degree is hardly the same as being sent to prison.

Roughly half of black families own their homes. More than one-fourth of African American adults work in management or professional jobs. Before the 2008 financial meltdown, African Americans had an aggregate purchasing power estimated at $913 billion.[8] If Mainstream black America were a sovereign nation, it would have the seventeenth-largest economy in the world—bigger than that of Turkey, for example, or Saudi Arabia, or South Africa. That all this has happened in the space of forty years, due to the ambition and labor of just two generations, is something of which Horatio Alger would be proud.

* * *

Why hasn't this Mainstream success penetrated the national consciousness? Mostly because we tend to see what we expect to see. Our eyes confirm what we "know," and everybody "knows" that black America is mired in intractable problems that defy solution. Everybody "knows" that black America, on average, has hardly begun to catch up with the rest of society—and since we "know" this, there is no reason to look more closely. If people would actually open their eyes, the existence of an enormous black Mainstream would be obvious. In terms of population and income, it's almost like failing to notice the existence of Australia.

It's hard to believe that half a century after Ralph Ellison's *Invisible Man* was published we'd still be talking about invisibility. But we are. Remember the conservative commentator Bill O'Reilly's famous dinner in September 2007 with the Reverend Al Sharpton at Sylvia's, the upscale soul-food restaurant in Harlem? Afterward, O'Reilly shared his amazement—there's no other word to describe it—with his radio audience. He marveled that "all the people up there are tremendously respectful." He gushed, "I couldn't get over the fact that there was no difference between Sylvia's restaurant and any other restaurant in New York City. I mean, it was exactly the same, even though it's run by blacks, primarily black patronship."

One wondered how, in O'Reilly's imagination, a black-owned restaurant in a black-majority neighborhood might deviate from the standard restaurant template. He explained: "There wasn't one person in Sylvia's who was screaming, 'M-Fer, I want more iced tea.' You know, I mean, everybody was—it was like going into an Italian restaurant in an all-white suburb in the sense of people were sitting there, and they were ordering and having fun. And there wasn't any kind of craziness at all."

He didn't stop there: "I think black Americans are starting to think more and more for themselves. They're getting away from the Sharptons and the [Reverend Jesse] Jacksons and the people trying to lead them into a race-based culture. They're just trying to figure it out. 'Look, I can make it. If I work hard and get educated, I can make it.' "9

Commentators, including me, had great fun at O'Reilly's expense. The remarks were outrageous, insulting, clueless, racist—all you had to do was pick a few loaded adjectives and fire away. There was another way to look at it, though. O'Reilly may be a bag of wind, but he's an intelligent bag of wind. He's not a Rush Limbaugh or a Glenn Beck or a Sean Hannity—not an entertainer who manipulates anger for ratings and wouldn't know how to engage with the issues in any serious way. I think O'Reilly is wrong about most everything, but I'm confident that if I visited his house I'd find actual shelves of actual books that he had actually read.

That such a man would be so utterly ignorant of the existence of the black Mainstream—not in Atlanta or Chicago, not somewhere deep in flyover country, but in the most famous black neighborhood in the nation, just blocks uptown from his studio—is astonishing. It's not just that he wouldn't have thought of venturing into a black Mainstream context without an escort. It's that, apparently, he had no idea that such a thing as the black Mainstream even existed.

* * *

If O'Reilly or anyone else wanted to meet the black Mainstream in a setting where outsiders rarely venture, I'd suggest going to homecoming weekend on a historically black college campus. The last time a visit to see my family happened to coincide with South Carolina State University's homecoming, I went to the game. When someone asked me about it later, I was able to report that the contest had been a squeaker, with the home team winning after several lead changes and momentum shifts. But for the life of me I couldn't recall who the opponent was. And I hadn't been drinking.

A friend of mine who lives in Washington—an SCSU graduate who retired not long ago after running a successful engineering consulting firm for many years—drives down to homecoming every year without fail, and never sets foot inside the stadium. He never even bothers to buy a ticket. If you were to conduct a survey asking what the point of SCSU's homecoming is, watching football would score pretty low. Watching halftime would score higher. The normal pattern is reversed: The stands actually *fill* when the second quarter ends, only to thin out again when the third quarter begins. Nobody wants to miss the spectacle.

The year I went, there was a controversy about the other team's cheerleaders, who were not just scantily and suggestively clad but whose routine included a lot of bumping, grinding, pelvis-thrusting, and booty-bouncing. "They look like a bunch of hoochie mamas," was the consensus of the women sitting in my row; the men wisely kept their opinions to themselves. SCSU's cheerleaders were only marginally more demure, however, and their performance only slightly less sexual. The advent of dance-troupe cheerleading squads that look as if they've escaped from a hip-hop music video is a hotly debated innovation in black-college football, but everybody's doing it.

Halftime's main event was the traditional battle of the marching bands. The visitors, who were from Norfolk State University in Virginia—I looked it up—performed first, and they were good. Surprisingly good. No one ever goes to a football game between historically black colleges expecting to hear a bad marching band, but Norfolk State momentarily stunned the crowd. SCSU has one of the nation's elite bands. The Marching 101 are expected to blow the competition away, not barely win the musical showdown. But that's what happened: a narrow victory, owing to more sophisticated choreography, tighter formations, and richer sound.

After halftime, people started drifting away to where the real action was. Sprawled across an area large enough to accommodate several football fields that cool, rainy Saturday afternoon was a soggy but high-spirited encampment. There were huge, Winnebago-style RVs, most with awnings that unfurled from the sides or the rear to provide shelter. There were pickup trucks with trailers on which were mounted barbecue grills large enough to cook a whole pig. There were hundreds and hundreds of cars, of course—SUVs, mostly, but also luxury cars, politically correct hybrids, the occasional vintage Mustang or Corvette. Everywhere there were party tents, some emblazoned with Greek letters signifying a fraternity or sorority. Vendors had set up tables to sell T-shirts, hats, and various tchotchkes. This was 2008, just a few weeks before the presidential election, and merchandise with the SCSU logo was running a poor second to anything labeled Obama.

Oh, and the people: thousands of men and women who belong to the black Mainstream, an unseen majority.

The invisibility of the black middle class is by now a standard trope of modern media criticism, but the phenomenon persists. Black dysfunction has always been newsworthy. Black achievement gets reported because those stories make everyone feel better, score points with black readers or viewers, and partly compensate for all the coverage of black dysfunction. Black normalcy is no more surprising, shocking, or heartwarming than any other color of normalcy, so it's really no surprise that it doesn't make the front page. But Mainstream black Americans seldom make the inside pages, either—the feature stories, for example, that are about neighborhood disputes over speed bumps, as opposed to neighborhood disputes about drug gangs.

There are black college professors who spend their professional lives studying international relations, but they aren't the experts that newspaper reporters and television producers keep on speed dial to offer wisdom about the latest crisis in Honduras or East Timor. There are black scuba clubs that jet off to explore the coast of Belize or the Great Barrier Reef, but their members aren't featured in stories about the impact of climate change on sensitive coral populations. There are African American motorcycle clubs that occasionally get written about, but only in a look-at-this, man-bites-dog sort of way; the president of Atlanta's biggest organized group of black Harley-Davidson riders would be quoted in a story whose point was how interesting it is that such a club exists but almost surely wouldn't be called for comment about a new mandatory helmet law.

In part, this is because society finds it so difficult to see the black experience as universal. For that matter, society has a hard time seeing anything other than what is considered the majority experience as universal. It caused not a ripple when Supreme Court justice Samuel Alito, in his Senate confirmation hearings, spoke of how his heritage as a descendant of Italian immigrants had a positive impact on the way he approached cases as an appellate judge. "Old country" roots, family passage through Ellis Island, hard-won assimilation, a sense of ethnic solidarity—that story, specific to only a minority of citizens, is seen as a quintessentially American narrative. But Justice Sonia Sotomayor, in her confirmation hearings, was scolded, excoriated, and accused of un-American bias over a years-old speech in which she mused about how her heritage as a "wise Latina" might make her a better judge. The Nuyorican narrative is one that the nation seems to have more trouble accepting as legitimately American, for some reason. Imagine the uproar that would have ensued if Barack Obama, during the campaign, had claimed that his African American heritage would make him a better president. Remember the uproar that *did* ensue when videotapes surfaced of the Reverend Jeremiah Wright, in flowing robes and full rhetorical flight, presenting an Afrocentric narrative of the country he had served honorably as a U.S. Marine.

This societal chauvinism is absurd, frustrating, at times even infuriating. I've appeared dozens of times on television with the conservative commentator Pat Buchanan and managed to keep my cool, but the one time I lost it—my eyes got round and crazy, friends say, and apparently I looked as if I were about to smack him—was when he adamantly, even aggressively refused to acknowledge my point that Sotomayor's personal history was every bit as American as his own. He's an intelligent man who reads books and knows history, but he could not bring himself to admit that a Puerto Rican girl's childhood in the Bronx was just as red, white, and blue as an Irish American boy's childhood in Washington. What made me berserk was that Buchanan wasn't just taking an extreme position for the sake of debate. He genuinely didn't get it.

The notion that there's something privileged and somehow sacred about the many variations of the Euro-Caucasian experience in America is destined to fade away. By 2045 or perhaps earlier, depending on which projection you believe, there will be no racial or ethnic majority in the United States.[10] We will be a huge and varied collection of minorities. This is already the case in our most populous states, California and Texas, and soon may be true in New York as well. White is right as a fundamental assumption, with or without racist intent, cannot possibly be long for this nation—or for this world, if you consider reasonable projections about the rise of China, India, Brazil, and other fast-developing nations that are not European or Anglo-American. But chauvinism is only one reason why the black middle-class experience is so seldom recognized as universal.

The other is the "two worlds" reality—the fact that we tend to keep so much of the black Mainstream experience to ourselves.

At the SCSU homecoming, a man who was selling Obama paraphernalia recognized me from my television appearances and called me over. He offered to give me a T-shirt, my choice of color. "I might give you two if you're a Q," he said.

"I didn't pledge," I told him, "but my father's an Alpha."

"Well, then, I don't know about this whole thing," he said playfully. "I always liked what you had to say when you were up there with Chris Matthews and Keith Olbermann, but I might have to do a reevaluation."

Translation: By asking about my being a Q, he was inquiring whether I was a member of the African American fraternity Omega Psi Phi. The Greek letter omega looks a bit like a capital Q that someone neglected to close at the bottom. Members often have the letter branded on one shoulder—literally burned into the skin with a branding iron, leaving a raised omega-shaped scar. Omega Psi Phi is one of the two most prominent black fraternities; the other is Alpha Phi Alpha, to which my late father belonged. Wherever you find a critical mass of college-educated black men, and I mean *wherever*, you'll find some Qs and some Alphas—and they'll be engaged in friendly, trash-talking rivalry. If your father was a Q, and you decide to pledge, then you naturally become a Q as well. The fraternity system is stronger on historically black campuses, but it's alive and well at white-majority schools as well. Alpha Phi Alpha was founded in 1906 at Cornell, and my father pledged while he was at the University of Michigan. If I hadn't arrived in Ann Arbor in 1970—a moment when the whole Greek thing seemed hopelessly out of touch with the social, cultural, and political revolution that was taking place—I'd surely have become an Alpha, too.

Similarly, sororities are an important lifelong affiliation for many college-educated black women. My mother is a member of Delta Sigma Theta, and naturally my sister, Ellen, when she arrived at Spelman College and decided to pledge, became a Delta, too. The trash-talking between Delta Sigma Theta and Alpha Kappa Alpha—which, truth be told, is the oldest black sorority, predating the Deltas by three years—is more demure than what you hear among the guys, but the rivalry is there just the same. Deltas have a thing about the color red. Whenever you're at an event with a lot of middle-class black women and you notice a statistically significant overabundance of red dresses, you're almost surely among a bunch of Deltas.

Aretha Franklin and Nikki Giovanni are Deltas. Dionne Warwick belongs to another sorority, Zeta Phi Beta. Toni Morrison is an Alpha Kappa Alpha, as was Marian Anderson. Martin Luther King Jr. and W. E. B. DuBois were Alphas. Bill Cosby, Vernon Jordan, and Michael Jordan are Qs, as were Langston Hughes and Roy Wilkins. These are lifelong affiliations, and while some men and women take them more seriously than others, few who have pledged a black fraternity or sorority take the commitment lightly. When African Americans speak of someone as "my fraternity brother" or "my sorority sister," a connection and even an obligation are implied.

There is nothing secretive or sinister, nothing skull-and-bones-ish about any of these organizations. They were established, beginning about a hundred years ago, to provide mutual support and encouragement among blacks who knew that when they graduated from college they would be taking their hard-won learning into a cruel, openly racist world. Obviously the world today is a different place. But the black fraternities and sororities have endured—and they have remained black.

There's one more African American fraternity I should mention. It isn't a campus affiliation but instead can only be joined—invitation only—by grown men: Sigma Pi Phi, known colloquially as the Boule, from an archaic Greek word meaning "representative assembly." The Boule (pronounced boo-lay) is for high-achieving black professionals, and its reach is nationwide. Once in Sacramento, which few would think of as a magnet for African Americans, my wife, Avis, and I were invited as guests to a Boule Sunday-afternoon get-together. The venue was the expansive, Spanish-colonial style home of a prominent young developer who was serving a term as head of the local Boule chapter. Present were college professors, former campus radicals, doctors, lawyers, financiers, and the like, along with their equally accomplished spouses. The only items on the agenda were food and fellowship. There was talk about the recession and its impact on the California real estate market. There was a certain amount of networking, I suppose, although these were men and women who had known one another long enough to have already made all the possible connections. The real point of the gathering was to gather—to laugh, commiserate, solve the problems of the world, debate the prospects of the Sacramento Kings, and agree on tee times for the coming week. There was something warm and almost womb-like about the afternoon—easy comfort in a house full of total strangers. There was so much we knew about one another's lives without even having to ask.

Everyone present was black. This slice of Mainstream black life—like so much of the cake—is for us. Not for anybody else.

* * *

Also, it may not be for long.

The us-against-the-world solidarity of Mainstream black culture is dissipating. On balance, it's hard to argue that this is a bad thing. In fact, it's hard to argue that it's not tremendously encouraging, given our nation's history with race. If there's no longer a bunker mentality, that must mean that those once in the bunker no longer feel themselves under attack. What's happening is assimilation, which is an odd term to use about a group whose first members landed before the *Mayflower*. It seems wrong to speak of assimilating into a society we literally helped build, counterintuitive to think of learning a culture to which we so lavishly contributed. But that's where the black Mainstream is headed—not this generation, perhaps, but surely the next.

My generation, like those that came before, was forged in an all-black context amid a hostile society. I went to all-black schools until integration, at which point I became a member of an embattled black clique. In higher education, the nation was reaching a tipping point: Before, most African Americans had attended historically black colleges and universities, but I graduated high school at a moment when white-majority institutions were actively seeking to attract black students. Today, only about 20 percent of black college students are attending historically black colleges and universities[11]—a complete reversal within just a few decades.

My wife and I grew up in black neighborhoods; one result of integration is that our sons did not. Most of the friends they had while growing up were white. But times had changed, and what we once thought of as "proprietary" black culture had spread beyond any narrow racial context. Black became not just acceptable but cool. Both of my sons have had white friends who spoke Ebonics much more fluently than they did. Likewise, young African Americans are acculturated and can easily converse in today's dialects of Valleyspeak. In black-majority

Mainstream community like Prince George's or DeKalb, it is not impossible for white kids to be cool and popular. And it is likely that black students, even if they grow up in mostly black or all-black neighborhoods, will eventually find themselves on white-majority college campuses. The lifelong friends they meet in the dorms will be white, Asian, Latino—the law of averages says they're unlikely to be black. When these Mainstream kids go out with their friends to hear music, it will be in integrated venues—not an all-black nightclub like the Bohemian Caverns of old. My generation had many of these world-expanding college experiences, too. But we had lived through the civil rights movement, the assassination of Dr. King, the riots, the emergence of the Black Panthers . . . We had the kind of race consciousness that comes from experience, not a history book.

All of which is a long way of saying that race doesn't matter to our children's generation in the same way it does to ours. It matters less. Change is good. But even welcome, long-awaited changes aren't easy.

For example, teenage angst and rebellion are innovations that Mainstream black America has found hard to accept. When there was a single black America, one of its cultural characteristics was respect for elders. It's not that teenagers or young adults always obeyed their parents—far from it—or that they didn't argue. But most of the insubordination was surreptitious. You did not sass your parents to their faces, no matter how unreasonable the command or how unjust the punishment you were being forced to endure. Once out of the house, of course, you did what you pleased. But you didn't provoke a confrontation. And if a direct confrontation did take place, you knew that even if you were absolutely right on the merits, you were still in the wrong for having forced the issue instead of finding some other way of making your point. You also did not sulk, mope, or whine like the sulky, mopey, whiny white teenagers you saw on television. From what we could tell, it seemed as if black juvenile delinquents were more respectful to their parents than white honor students were to theirs.

Now, Mainstream parents are often confronted with the kind of sassing, sulking, whining, and moping that their own parents never would have tolerated. Perhaps this is an inevitable step in the assimilation process, analogous to young Indian Americans who refuse to go along with arranged marriages, or young Korean Americans who balk at joining the family business. It is a less profound form of rebellion than those other examples. But it frustrates parents and sometimes strains family bonds in a way that many African Americans find alien and distressing.

Another adjustment for Mainstream parents is that the girlfriends and boyfriends their children bring home from high school or college may not be African American. This sets up a conflict between two strongly held Mainstream values—on one side an absolute belief in Dr. King's dream that all be judged solely by the content of their character, on the other a fierce determination that African American history and culture be not only revered but also perpetuated.

Mainstream black America, then, seems in many ways a paradoxical place. We demanded and won the right to live wherever we want, but many of us decide to live together in clumps. We complain, with justification, that the nation seems not to know or acknowledge that middle-class black Americans even exist, but we conduct much of middle-class black

American life out of the larger society's field of vision. We marched, studied, and worked our way to the point where we are assimilating, but we have reservations about assimilation if it means giving up our separate identity.

For the Mainstream, race shouldn't matter. But it does.

5 THE ABANDONED: NO WAY OUT

I've seen the Reverend Jesse Jackson rendered speechless exactly twice. The second time was the night Barack Obama was elected president, and Jackson stood among the multitudes in Chicago's Grant Park, silent tears of joy streaming down his face.

The first time was three years earlier, in drowned, desperate New Orleans.

I had decided that I couldn't watch the unfolding Hurricane Katrina catastrophe on television any longer. I had to see it for myself, and I had to write about it. So I caught a flight to Baton Rouge, rented a minivan—I wanted an SUV, but for obvious reasons they were in great demand—and headed off down the interstate toward a city I'd last seen when I was in college and a bunch of us had decided to see what Mardi Gras was all about. I knew that the first post-flood evacuation flights out of the submerged city were supposed to leave that day, so I found my way to Louis Armstrong New Orleans International Airport. As I neared the terminal, it was as if I had suddenly been transported to some other country.

With more than a quarter of a mile to go, I drove past the end of a long line of people who looked like third world refugees. They bristled at that description, I later learned. They were citizens of what we insist is the greatest country on earth, they were beneficiaries in good standing of vaunted American exceptionalism, and the greatest country on earth would not allow any force, natural or man-made, to reduce its citizens to the helpless, pathetic status of refugees. The greatest country on earth would not countenance the scene I saw that day: thousands of people, virtually all of them black, carrying everything they owned on their backs or in battered suitcases, shuffling forward inch by inch in a sad, silent queue to be put on military aircraft that would take them somewhere, anywhere, as far as possible from the hellhole into which fate had plunged them. It wasn't something that anyone would ever see in America. Yet here we were.

I parked near the long, crescent-shaped terminal and rapped on the first door I came to; like all the rest, it was guarded by uniformed personnel wielding automatic weapons. My press pass got me inside, and immediately I had second thoughts. The smell was overpowering: waste, decay, death. The terminal was dim, still mostly without power, and it took awhile for my eyes to adjust. What was normally a soaring atrium, meant to be evocative of glorious flight, had been converted into a field hospital—a MASH unit, like on the old television show but without the gallows humor. There were rows of cots occupied by patients. All that I could see were black, all were elderly, and some appeared to be in extremis. I buttonholed a doctor, and he gave me a status report: A few overwhelmed physicians and nurses were trying to care for hundreds of very sick people. They had no medical histories to guide them. In the many cases involving some degree of dementia, they couldn't even be sure of the patient's name. They weren't able to diagnose, only guess; and whether they guessed right or wrong, there wasn't much they could do except make the patient as comfortable as possible. Even basic medicines were lacking, including insulin—and the doctor was certain that many, if not most, of the men and women on those cots were diabetic. A man on a nearby cot was gasping for breath; the doctor asked if someone could please try to find a functioning oxygen tank.

I had to get away from the smell, so I walked through the atrium to the next segment of the long terminal. This was where that wretched line I'd seen on the way into the airport eventually led—past deserted ticket counters and shuttered souvenir shops to a gate and a jetway, somewhere on a far concourse, that led to a flight. Who knew where the plane would be going. At this point, who cared?

Katrina and its aftermath shocked the nation not only because of the fearsome meteorology we witnessed but also because of the shocking demography. That there existed large numbers of African Americans who are not middle class in income or outlook was something the nation knew, but for many people this fact had become increasingly abstract— useful as a statistic to cite in arguments about affirmative action, education policy, or national competitiveness, but not necessarily a relevant fact of daily life.

Katrina gave the numbers flesh and bone and blood. And voice: *We're still here.*

At the airport, I was watching Abandoned black Americans being uprooted, traumatized, and driven away in what looked almost like a pogrom. I took out a notebook and began interviewing people, and the first words I wrote were "state of shock"—that's where they all appeared to be. Every family whose privacy I invaded had a harrowing story of escape and survival. One woman told me how the water seemed to rise a foot each minute, how she and her husband ran upstairs and then climbed into the attic, how he used a hammer to make a hole that let them clamber onto the roof, how the two of them escaped the Lower Ninth Ward in a neighbor's boat, how they paddled and waded and finally walked the miles to the Ernest N. Morial Convention Center downtown, and how they had endured three days there with no food or water except what strangers offered to share. One man said, with emotionless affect, that his family had become separated in the chaotic scramble; he had no idea where the others might be, but was sure they were all right. Another man was carrying one suitcase and his camera bag. He had lost everything else, he said, but he was proud of having saved the camera because he was convinced that the pictures he took during the flood would prove that "they"—he meant officials who were acting on behalf of those citizens who happened to be affluent, powerful, and, not incidentally, white—had deliberately sacrificed poor black neighborhoods like the Lower Ninth by dynamiting certain levees in order to save the famous French Quarter and the wealthy Garden District. The man had shot film, not digital, so he couldn't show me the photographic evidence. I gave him my card but never heard from him.

A retired teacher named John Mullen III told me of one detail he remembered from the long hours he spent on top of his house in the Lower Ninth Ward: "There were redfish in the water, and they were coming up to eat the cockroaches at the water line." It wasn't the image that stuck with him but the sound—a little slurp—and he couldn't get it out of his head.

I made my way slowly toward the front of the line, but after a while I stopped doing interviews. I couldn't process any more loss, couldn't bring myself to force any more broken families to talk about the dead and the missing. I needed air, so I ducked out the nearest door—and quite literally bumped into Reverend Jackson, who had arrived in the disaster zone earlier that day. He was standing there, looking at the people in the line, the ambulances still arriving, the heavily armed National Guard troops, the exhaustion on the faces of victims and samaritans alike. A local news crew had spotted him and rushed over, certain he would offer a good sound bite. But one of the great talkers of our time had nothing to say. He and I greeted each other, then stood in silence for a while. There were no words.

The waters in New Orleans flushed out a long-ignored residue of black poverty and dysfunction for all to see. The nation felt a deep sense of shame, at least for a while. But the reality of Abandoned black America had been there all along—perfectly visible to those who cared to look.

Before the flood, two-thirds of New Orleans's population was black. The city was one of the poorest in the country; the official poverty rate was a staggering 27.9 percent, according to the authoritative Greater New Orleans Community Data Center, and some 84 percent of those poor people were African American.[1] Nearly half of African Americans with incomes below the poverty line lived in neighborhoods where the poverty rate exceeded 40 percent, according to a Brookings Institution analysis—which meant that poverty was highly concentrated.[2]

In other words, the racially segregated but economically integrated model for African American neighborhoods until the 1960s had given way to a new model—still racially segregated, as far as the Abandoned were concerned, but now economically segregated as well. In New Orleans as elsewhere, concentrated black poverty was accompanied by concentrated black dysfunction. Four out of every five children in these neighborhoods were being raised in single-parent households. Only three out of five working-age adults actually participated in the labor market. Just one adult in twelve, in these Abandoned zones, had a college degree.[3]

The upwardly mobile black Mainstream was steadily moving out, either to the suburbs or to a newly developed sector of the city called New Orleans East. As the black population became poorer and less educated, it became more resentful. Mayor Ray Nagin, whose histrionics during and after the flood drew nationwide ridicule, had won election in the first place because he had the backing of whites, middle-class blacks, and the powerful downtown business community. His credentials as a longtime corporate executive provoked more suspicion than admiration in Abandoned neighborhoods—places where people would notice the *thunk* of car doors locking when a black corporate executive, perhaps having lost his way, rolled through in his shiny BMW or Benz.

There is no excuse for the behavior of the young men and women who, when the hurricane hit, rushed downtown to loot the stores. It is useful, though, to have a sense of how they viewed the world. For most Americans, New Orleans is synonymous with fun. The city's insomniac street-party culture is, indeed, unique and enchanting. But in Abandoned neighborhoods like Mid-City, Treme, and the Lower Ninth, the good times did not roll. The public schools were failing so hopelessly that a whole generation was effectively being written off. The exodus of the oil and gas industry was almost complete, which meant there were precious few jobs to be had except in the low-paying tourism sector. Drug dealing was what passed for economic development in some neighborhoods. Black-on-black crime was a truly horrific problem—the city's murder rate regularly flirted with being the highest in the nation—and it seemed as if all the police wanted to do was contain the fire, not put it out. The authorities' main concern seemed to be making sure that violent criminals were kept away from the restaurants, casinos, strip clubs, and trinket shops of the tourist zone, lest the city's theme-park image suffer.

So the breakdown of order that Hurricane Katrina caused was more than an opportunity to steal. It was a chance for payback—not against any individual, not against any one retailer, but against a whole system. The rampage, such as it was, proved highly impractical. When the streets are under six feet of water, another name for "wide-screen TV" is "not-very-good raft."

At the airport and elsewhere, it was the Abandoned who insisted on the theory—which was baseless—that poor neighborhoods had been intentionally flooded so that rich neighborhoods could stay dry. I spoke with at least a dozen people who swore they had heard the explosions that demolished the floodwalls protecting the Lower Ninth. In fact, there were no explosions; the witnesses probably heard ships, houses, concrete slabs, and other flotsam being smashed around by the inrushing torrent. After I got back to Washington from covering the flood, I accepted an invitation to appear on Fox News for the first (and last) time. Bill O'Reilly used a column I had written as an excuse to ridicule the idea that anyone could think, even for one minute, that government officials would do such a thing as deliberately and callously flood American citizens out of house and home. I informed him that within the living memory of some of those Lower Ninth Ward residents, government officials had done just that: At the height of the Great Mississippi Flood of 1927, authorities dynamited levees south of New Orleans, ruining farmhouses and destroying crops, in a desperate and misguided attempt to save the city. O'Reilly paused for a nanosecond, then responded that, well, he didn't know about any of that . . . but he *did* know that it was an *outrage* that people would *think* such a thing, and that it was *irresponsible* for a journalist to report that people were saying such *nonsense*. As I said, that was my one appearance on Fox.

There was near-universal criticism of how Mayor Nagin handled the evacuation of the city in the hours before Katrina made landfall, but in many ways he orchestrated a great success; the vast majority of New Orleanians heeded the warnings and managed to get out. The early evacuees, however, included most whites, most middle-class blacks, and a much smaller percentage of the poor. Those Abandoned black Americans who remained had been literally abandoned: They found themselves, basically, the only people left in town. The impression conveyed by much of the television coverage was of a bunch of poor black people who were too ignorant to get out of the path of the storm of the century—and who then, trapped in a Waterworld without laws or authority, reverted to savagery.

I knew better. The day after my trip to the New Orleans airport, I was back in the city—this time in the French Quarter, which had remained dry. I heard a breathless report on the radio warning people to steer clear of the Jackson Square area because a sniper was on the loose; police were said to be pinned down under heavy fire. That was odd, because I happened to be a block away, and I'd seen no evidence of trouble. I went over to the square and asked some loitering police officers about the "sniper," and they looked at me as if I were hallucinating. They had been there all morning. They were in communication with their colleagues around the Quarter. Nothing of the sort had happened.

There were reports of people firing at rescue helicopters—untrue, as far as I could determine. There had indeed been instances in which people stranded on their roofs fired weapons, but the flood victims I talked to said the shooters were trying to get the attention of the helicopters, not bring them down.

If you think about it, that's the only explanation that makes sense. But fear of the unleashed black unknown was not conducive to clear thinking. Rumors of phantom snipers led hapless federal officials—under the leadership of the feckless Federal Emergency Management Agency chief Michael Brown—to organize their rescue crews into huge armored convoys comprising scores of vehicles. A convoy would set out in some direction, and the lead truck would inevitably reach a point where the water was too deep to proceed. Then an hour or more would be wasted while the whole convoy was turned around and pointed in some other direction. Soon the lead vehicle would reach deep water again, and the whole process had to be repeated. Precious time and resources were being squandered, all because of reports that somewhere, hiding in the ruined city, there might be poor African Americans with guns.

There were, indeed, many incidents of criminal violence— New Orleans was, after all, no stranger to crime before the flood. But I watched as young men wearing the "fear me" uniform—baggy pants around the hips, white T-shirts, cheap gold chains—helped distribute bottled water to exhausted families. I saw human beings pulling together to get through a crisis, just as human beings do all over the world.

There is no one explanation for how so many people ended up staying rather than leaving. It's true that transportation was a major factor for some. Anyone who didn't own a car, and couldn't get a ride from someone who did own one, was basically out of luck. By the time it had become clear that a once-in-a-lifetime hurricane strike was almost certain, as opposed to merely possible, other modes of getting out of town—planes, trains, buses—had ceased operating and moved their equipment to safety. Perhaps if Nagin had pressed all the city's school buses into service, thousands more might have escaped the storm. But that's not the kind of elaborate contingency plan that can be put together in an hour or two. Qualified drivers would have had to know when and where to report for duty. Would-be evacuees would have had to know to gather at pre-identified pick-up points. And, of course, there would have had to be someplace for the buses to go once they left New Orleans.

Most of the people I spoke with, though, had other reasons

for deciding to hunker down. An unusually high percentage of poor African Americans in New Orleans own their homes rather than rent, and some were determined to protect their property against looting. The parts of the Lower Ninth Ward that are closest to the Mississippi sit on relatively high ground, and those streets had never flooded before Katrina; I met one man who made the reasonable, but unlucky, wager that history would prove a good guide. Several people told me that they had had the means to leave, but could find no way to safely move their elderly relatives who were housebound with chronic medical problems.

Like those who evacuated, those who stayed behind had chosen from among their viable options. They just had fewer of them.

* * *

How did those options become so very narrow? The story involves several interwoven narratives.[4] Hurricane Katrina offers an apt analogy, in that it was literally a "perfect storm" whose devastating impact depended on the synergy of unrelated factors. A canal built years ago to shorten the shipping route to the Gulf of Mexico hadn't been properly maintained, and as a result had widened greatly. As the hurricane neared, its winds blew at just the right angle to send a massive surge of water coursing toward the city; ultimately that surge helped overwhelm the floodwalls that were supposed to protect the Lower Ninth Ward. Then, as the storm continued inland, it narrowly missed hitting New Orleans head-on, instead passing a few miles to the east; this meant that while the hurricane had approached from the south, the most powerful winds, those closest to the eye, swirled in from the north. Those winds sent water from Lake Pontchartrain into several drainage canals that puncture the city like daggers, putting unbearable pressure on the thin floodwalls that ran alongside the canals. When those barriers failed, water from the lake, which is at a higher elevation than most of the city, poured in. All of these factors had to combine in just the right—or wrong—way for New Orleans to be turned into a giant bathtub with no drain. Likewise, it took a conspiracy of woe to create the human conditions that Hurricane Katrina unmasked.

In the 1950s, the Lower Ninth Ward was a working-class, mostly black community. By the time Katrina hit, the modifiers "working-class" and "mostly" no longer applied. Half of all households in the neighborhood reported income of less than $20,000 a year, according to the 2000 census, with only about 13 percent earning more than $50,000 annually. More than 98 percent of the Lower Ninth Ward's residents were black.[5]

On a return visit to New Orleans four months after the flood, I met a cheerful and determined woman in her fifties named Janie Blackmon, who was working with a preservationist group to try to bring the ruined neighborhood back to life. She had grown up in Holy Cross, the part of the district nearest the Mississippi, and remembered when the Lower Ninth was home not exclusively to African American families like hers but also to a smattering of Italians and Jews. There was a thriving commercial strip, but not much industry; the Lower Ninth was a place where families owned their homes, where fathers got up every morning, said goodbye to the wife and kids, went to their jobs elsewhere in the city, and came home at night to a hot supper. Blackmon pointed to houses where the same families had lived for four or five generations. Everyone knew the big house where the Lower Ninth's most famous resident lived: the legendary musician Antoine Dominique "Fats" Domino. He stayed—and survived Katrina. Everything else changed.

Those working-class jobs that had sustained the Lower Ninth disappeared. The acclaimed sociologist William Julius Wilson, now at Harvard and formerly at the University of Chicago, was a pioneer in studying the evolution of persistent black poverty in inner cities across the nation. Wilson argued in favor of the "spatial mismatch" theory that the migration of industry—indeed, of most economic growth—from central urban zones to the suburbs and beyond was the principal factor in the creation of what is sometimes called the black underclass. With few jobs available nearby for low-skilled or entry-level workers, with transportation a daunting ordeal for anyone without a car, and with no easy way for inner-city residents even to learn of employment opportunities in the burgeoning suburbs, joblessness in neighborhoods like the Lower Ninth Ward soared.

That would seem to be the obvious consequence. But Wilson argued that the disappearance of work opportunities had another effect: Young women concluded they had little incentive to marry the fathers of their children, since the men were now unlikely to become steady breadwinners. Mothers decided they could do as well, or perhaps better, raising the children on their own. The result was that the two-parent household became just one of several possible living arrangements, rather than a standard enforced by the moral judgment of friends and neighbors. The single-parent, female-headed household—once considered a shameful way to live—became commonplace, then normal.[6]

Wilson's work is often cited as an answer to the theory,

espoused by some conservatives, that welfare payments targeted at helping mothers who were living without male partners created an even clearer economic incentive for women not to marry. Those looking for a noneconomic explanation for the decline of the traditional nuclear family in Abandoned black America have often pointed to the dearth of sex education and the infrequency of condom use among African American teens. But when a Pulitzer Prize–winning colleague of mine at *The Washington Post*, the journalist Leon Dash, spent a year living in one of Washington's most distressed housing projects, he found that the young girls who became pregnant were not confused in the least about how babies were made, and that condoms were readily accessible. Dash found that girls made the conscious decision to become pregnant for a variety of reasons. Single motherhood was often a multigenerational phenomenon. Some girls felt confined living with their mothers and siblings, and knew that having a baby would allow them to establish their own households—perhaps in a subsidized apartment just a courtyard away. Others were responding to a less practical but far deeper need for proprietorship: in a transient and precarious world, the sense that *I made this and it will always be mine.*

Whatever the principal reason, the phenomenon itself is undeniable. When Katrina hit the Lower Ninth, well over half of all households with children under eighteen were headed by a woman with no husband present. Only about 25 percent of children were living in households with both parents—about the same as the percentage of children in the Lower Ninth who were being raised not by a parent but by their *grandparents.*[7] The traditional family had broken down.

Other scholars have argued that "spatial mismatch" alone

is not enough to explain how neighborhoods like the Lower Ninth devolved into the islands of extreme poverty and dysfunction that constitute the archipelago of Abandoned black America. At the same time that jobs were moving out of the cities, African Americans were winning unprecedented rights and freedoms. Those who were best prepared to take advantage of the new opportunities moved away from places like the Lower Ninth, leaving the least-prepared behind. The 1960s riots hastened an exodus that had already begun. As the black Mainstream made for the exit, what had been economically diverse African American neighborhoods became uniformly poor.

Out-migration of the Mainstream doesn't seem to explain the full extent of the transformation, however. Some studies indicate that a greater effect may be produced by the movement of poor African Americans—people who, for whatever reason, have to find a new place to live. Poor black people, when they move, are likely to move into neighborhoods that are poorer and more racially segregated than the neighborhoods they are leaving. So what happens is a kind of distillation that effectively cooks off the middle class and the working class until only the Abandoned remain.

At the same time, though, these "destination" neighborhoods have thinned out: Low density, compared to the pre–civil rights days, is characteristic of Abandoned zones throughout the country, with block after block dotted with derelict buildings and vacant lots, like the gaps in a six-year-old's smile. This winnowing has been taken to an extreme in Detroit and its satellite industrial cities such as Pontiac and Flint, where the big question now is which parts of town to let nature reclaim. Like most cities from which industry has fled, New Orleans before Katrina had a much bigger geographical footprint than it needed—the city's population was about 475,000, down from a peak of 627,000 in 1960.[8] The Lower Ninth Ward still had the fabric of a real neighborhood, but it was frayed and moth-eaten.

One last key factor in creating the conditions that Katrina exposed—the conditions in which Abandoned black America lives—is racial segregation. That sounds trivially obvious—in that we are considering black neighborhoods, not integrated ones—but it's not. All else being equal, we should expect to find poor black, white, and Hispanic people all living together in poor neighborhoods. But that is not the case. Princeton sociologist Douglas S. Massey argues that racial segregation is the most important factor in the concentration of black poverty because African Americans have fewer housing options and are especially hard-hit in any economic downturn.[9]

All these factors had conspired to set the scene for Katrina. They did their work like experienced stagehands—efficiently and out of sight.

* * *

One reason the scenes from devastated New Orleans were so shocking is that in many metropolitan areas, the inner city isn't what it used to be. Quite often, it isn't even *where* it used to be.

Across the country, gentrification has turned dangerous, decrepit, close-in, once exclusively black neighborhoods into hip oases where the most outrageous crime is what coffee shops charge for a few drops of espresso mixed with some warm milk. This transformation is far from complete, it must be said, and there are cities where you could drive around for hours and decide that it hasn't made much of a dent at all. In Chicago, for example, vast sectors of the South Side are still unreconstructed ghetto, while in Baltimore whole neighborhoods of once-tidy row houses are abandoned, boarded up, and rotting away—the postapocalyptic cityscape familiar to viewers of *The Wire*.

It is also the case that only when the real estate market is booming do blocks of Harlem brownstones become prettified, and only when it's *really* booming could a row of former crack dens in Washington metamorphose into a happening nightlife district, anchored by a chic bistro serving mussels, fries, and Belgian beer. When the housing market tanks, gentrification is put on hold. The process rarely goes into reverse, though. It works like a ratchet: Once seized, territory is seldom surrendered. Push by shove, eviction by foreclosure, poor people are moved from the center to the margins.

At the same time, the Abandoned are pushed to the margins of our consciousness. There was a time when the status of the poor was a much-debated issue in American public life, if only because the non-poor were so afraid of them. Crime was seen as such an urgent problem that a generation of politicians won office by promising "law and order"—which was shorthand, I would argue, for protecting the rich and white from the poor and black. Zero-tolerance policing was invented, "three-strikes" laws were passed, mandatory sentencing was imposed, and new prisons were built. A generation of young criminals either went straight, went to jail, or went to the grave, and the ultraviolent crack epidemic burned itself out. When was the last time any politician made "safer streets" the centerpiece of a campaign?

Since the early 1990s, the incidence of serious violent crime in the United States has fallen by nearly 40 percent, from 747 such offenses per 100,000 population in 1993 to 467 per 100,000 in 2007, according to the Census Bureau.[10] Some believe the decline is mostly a function of demographic trends; others credit the draconian laws and tough prison sentences; still others see a collateral benefit of economic growth. Whatever the cause—and despite the impression of unabated, rampant depravity and mayhem conveyed nightly by the eleven o'clock news—most people understand at some level that when they walk down the street these days, they have less reason to fear getting mugged than they did twenty years ago. Poverty simply isn't the menace it once was. Except in extraordinary circumstances—such as Hurricane Katrina—poverty just doesn't command the nation's attention the way it used to.

So to find Abandoned black America today, you have to look a bit harder. You have to go to the corners of cities, to neighborhoods often neatly bypassed by the freeways and avenues that commuters use to get downtown. You have to find your way into shabby little pockets of the inner suburbs, where refugees from gentrification have found precarious sanctuary. You have to travel to the rural South and visit communities where upward mobility is marked not by building a Mitchellville Mansion but by moving out of a shotgun shack into a reasonably new double-wide.

In Washington, the Abandoned have been pushed steadily eastward—and even out of town. In 1970, the city's population was 70 percent black; today, the African American majority is down to 54 percent, and it's still falling fast.[11] In 2009, for the first time since the advent of local government in a city ultimately ruled by Congress, a majority of the elected city council was white. The District of Columbia can be called Chocolate City no more.

Thirty years ago, the desirable Capitol Hill neighborhood was expensive, mostly white, and just a few blocks wide. During each successive real estate boom, imaginative realtors pushed the boundary of Capitol Hill first to the east, in increments of several blocks at a time, then north all the way to the H Street corridor, which since the riots had been considered one of the most dangerous places in town. These days, I have to admit that the sight of a young Caucasian couple pushing a baby stroller down artsy, avant-garde H Street gives me a jolt of cognitive dissonance. There was a time when I might have pulled over, asked if they had *any idea* where they were, and perhaps even offered them a lift. Then again, I might have done the same for a yuppified black couple, since H Street was an equal-opportunity mugging zone. One of its alleys was the scene of a particularly heinous crime: In 1984, a forty-eight-year-old African American woman named Catherine Fuller was horrifically raped and murdered by a gang of young men in what might have been a scene from *A Clockwork Orange*. Witnesses must have seen the attack and heard Fuller's screams, but nobody intervened. The killing was seen as a measure of the depths to which the city had fallen.

Today, Capitol Hill—the name, if not the elevation—extends all the way from the Capitol to the Anacostia River, a polluted, slow-moving estuarine tributary of the Potomac that cuts off nearly a third of the city from the rest. Row houses in the newly added precincts of Capitol Hill have been spruced up with all-stainless kitchens and polished hardwood floors. Decrepit old commercial buildings have been converted into faux-loft condos; Eastern Market, once an authentic place where locals went to buy everything from collard greens to crab cakes, has been turned into an "authentic" place catering mostly to people who couldn't tell a ham hock from a hog jowl if their lives depended on it. There are islands of poverty that remain, but they shrink year by year as longtime homeowners and landlords sell to developers with big ideas.

The Abandoned who lived on the flatland that Capitol Hill swallowed—like the Abandoned who lived around U Street, those who lived in the tenements around the industrial zone where developers built the city's new baseball stadium, those who lived in the suddenly trendy neighborhood north of Massachusetts Avenue (inevitably called NoMa), those who lived in riot-scarred, now-revitalized Columbia Heights, and many others—have largely been pushed across the river. Everyone knows that "the river" in question is not the Potomac but the Anacostia.

Most of the millions of tourists who visit the nation's capital probably have no idea that this remote part of the city even exists. People often refer to the whole area east of the river as "Anacostia," but actually it's a vast sector made up of many distinct neighborhoods—Congress Heights, Barry Farm, Deanwood. The small historic district that is properly called Anacostia is where the black abolitionist Frederick Douglass lived; his hilltop home is now a national historic site. The panorama from Douglass's front door is one of the best in town, with the Capitol, the Washington Monument, and the rest of the city's monumental core strewn at your feet; on the Fourth of July, it's as if the fireworks are for you alone. Such to-die-for views will inevitably attract hordes of gentrifying pioneers to what is an incongruously beautiful ghetto—heavily wooded, coursed with streams, dotted with parks—but so far the flow is a bare trickle. "East of the river" has always had pockets of Mainstream comfort, and they cling on. But it's the poorest and blackest part of town. It's where the Abandoned live.

It wasn't like that when I was growing up. Dorothy Fordham, a first cousin of my mother's, lived in a tidy house just off Alabama Avenue. She had a pioneering career as an officer in the army—few black women had ever advanced so far—and her stories of exotic postings and intrigue-filled assignments were fascinating. Aunt Dorothy remained in that little house after she retired, and the neighborhood slowly sank around her. Longtime neighbors died or moved away, to be replaced by newcomers with less regard for niceties such as landscaping and maintenance. They were less neighborly, too: A few years ago, already past eighty, she was attacked and badly bitten by a pit bull whose careless owner lived down the street. Never the type to be pushed around, she held her ground until an incapacitating stroke forced her into an assisted-living facility. Now that she's gone, what will happen to her immaculate house?

"Law and order" is very much an issue east of the river; people who are poor and black have always suffered disproportionately from violent crime, much of it committed by people who are black and poor. A popular pastime among young men who live in one big housing project is stealing cars—to go joy-riding around the city, to have drag races on a notorious strip of highway in Prince George's County, or perhaps just as a way to pass the time. Drug dealing is seen as a regular form of commerce in some neighborhoods—not accepted but expected. East of the river is where most of the city's handgun shootings and murders occur, frequently as a result of longstanding feuds between "crews"—that's the word local authorities use to avoid calling them gangs, because acknowledging a gang problem would mean having to do something about it. The crews are based in different neighborhoods, to which they are fiercely loyal. Often the bullets fly during battles over drug turf, but sometimes it's just because some guys from, say, Barry Farm were seen promenading around Congress Heights in a way that somehow conveyed disrespect. The origins of such territorial disputes are lost in the mists of time, but they are important enough that schoolteachers have to know which kids live where, so they can arrange their classroom seating in a way most likely to minimize conflict.

The pressures of the real estate market have begun to push the Abandoned and their attendant problems across the city line into Prince George's communities such as Capitol Heights. A jurisdiction proudly dominated by the black Mainstream is having to deal with an influx of crime, drugs, and violence—and has proved to be, generally, in no mood to make allowances for the socioeconomic disparities that give rise to criminality. Thirty years ago, the police force in Prince George's was overwhelmingly white and had a reputation for heavy-handed brutality in dealing with African Americans unlucky enough to be arrested in the county. Now, with the county under black leadership and the police force about half African American, the reputation persists—and many residents ignore, if not encourage, what remains of the old "ready, fire, aim" approach to fighting crime.

In Abandoned zones on both sides of the Anacostia, the Mainstream institutions that held out the longest were the churches. Before the Shaw neighborhood south of U Street began to gentrify, I remember that every Sunday morning the streets would be all but blocked by double-parked cars with Maryland license plates—parishioners who had moved out of the city but came back, once a week, out of loyalty to the churches they had grown up in and the pastors who had baptized them. But now those churches have begun to migrate to the suburbs—especially Prince George's—because that's where most of the membership lives. The traditional congregations have had to take this step for competitive reasons: Megachurches, mostly Pentecostal in nature, have sprung up in the county and siphoned thousands of members away from Baptist, African Methodist Episcopal, and other traditional denominations. One such place of worship, Jericho City of Praise, claims nineteen thousand members. The church runs its own Christian academy and a host of social-service programs.

On Sundays, the traffic flow is reversed: In the Jericho City of Praise parking lots you will find quite a few cars with District of Columbia license plates. Some of those cars belong to Abandoned black Americans who are convinced that although this life may be hard, the next life will be pure comfort and joy.

* * *

The web of restraints that keeps Abandoned black Americans from escaping into the middle class has been examined from every angle, described in great detail, and lamented ad infinitum. But the web continues to tighten.

It begins in the womb. Poor black women are only one-third as likely as poor white women to have adequate prenatal care. This is partly mitigated by the fact that poor black women are much less likely than their white counterparts to smoke while they are pregnant; indeed, rates of tobacco, alcohol, and drug

use among low-income young African Americans are generally lower than among low-income whites. Still, infant mor-
tality is almost twice as high among African Americans. The
incidence of low birth weight is also greatly elevated, and
while most studies do not show an ironclad, direct relationship between low birth weight and a decrease in cognitive
ability, they do indicate that low-birth-weight children are up
to twice as likely to have problems in school. From a very early
age, the children of the Abandoned are at much greater risk
for several chronic, debilitating conditions—asthma, obesity,
childhood diabetes—than low-income white children. Poor
black children are behind even before the race begins.

Most infants born into low-income African American families are, of course, of normal weight and go home from the
hospital in good health. But what kind of home?

In 1940, only 15.7 percent of African American households
nationwide were headed by women who were either single,
widowed, or abandoned by their spouses. In 1960, just 22 percent of black children were growing up in one-parent households. Today, an astounding 54 percent of all African American
children are being raised in single-parent households[12]—
and, in almost all cases, it's the father who is absent while the
mother struggles to take care of the family.

It is hugely significant that in most Abandoned black neighborhoods, as in the Lower Ninth Ward, most households are
headed by a single woman—with no husband on the prem-
ises. In many cases, both the mother and the absent father
were themselves raised by single mothers. To the extent that
the example set by parents provides a model for children to
emulate, girls grow up learning that it would be normal to
raise children on their own and boys learning that it would be

normal not to live with the mother—or mothers—of their children. The pattern tends to repeat in the next generation. Being a single parent is stressful, with the mother likely to pass that stress on to her children—along with all the well-documented physiological damage that stress can cause. The complex and subtle psychological impacts of single parenthood might be surpassed, however, by a simpler and more quantifiable economic impact: One low income provides approximately half as much money as two low incomes. This fact of arithmetic limits upward mobility. It also greatly increases instability because the slightest disruption of a household's one precarious source of cash can create a situation in which the family has to move on short notice. And if a single mother who lacks educational qualifications and marketable skills is fortunate enough to have a steady job, it is unlikely to pay enough for her to afford quality day care. Preschoolers are likely to be cared for by relatives, neighbors, or older siblings, and while these ad hoc caretakers are full of love and good intentions, they will rarely have the skills needed to optimize a child's early development. As a result of all these factors, children of Abandoned families are at a significant disadvantage, compared to their more affluent peers, when they enter school.

William Raspberry, my friend and former colleague at *The Washington Post*, decided when he retired that blazing a trail for younger African American journalists to follow, becoming one of the most widely read syndicated columnists in the country, and winning a Pulitzer Prize did not constitute enough of a contribution. So instead of taking up golf, he founded a nonprofit and set out to make a difference in his hometown of Okolona, Mississippi, a town of about 3,500 that is 60 percent black, mostly poor, and long since Abandoned.

Raspberry decided to focus on early-childhood education, which is where he thought the greatest return on his philanthropic investment could be made. He soon discovered, however, that before he could effectively educate young children, he had to educate their families. As he learned more, parents became his program's main focus.

Raspberry's program, called BabySteps, teaches parents how to prepare their children for success in school. Raspberry found that it wasn't enough to invite parents to sessions where they would be given instruction. Counselors make home visits to assess the parents' capacity and demonstrate model behaviors for them to imitate. As Raspberry once explained to me, it does little good to tell parents to read to their children every night if the parents are not capable of reading with any fluency; some boys and girls would be better off if they came regularly to a BabySteps facility where counselors could read to them. Raspberry then discovered that health was another major issue, and BabySteps ended up establishing a weekly health and dental clinic to serve the children of Okolona. This holistic approach seems to be producing real results. If there were a Bill Raspberry for every Abandoned community—and deep-pockets donors willing to fund programs like BabySteps, which costs more than half a million dollars a year—this would be a very different book.

Even if every young child in Abandoned black America had the best possible early preparation, most would encounter schools where expectations are low and performance is even lower. There is no need to describe in detail the abject failure of public education in poor inner-city and rural communities; everyone knows that tragic story by now, and at this point the only part anyone wants to read is the still-unwritten happy ending. I've spent enough time in such schools—as a reporter and columnist, and as a volunteer in a nonprofit college-access program that my wife, Avis, founded—to know that the few kids who overcome their surroundings, going on to success in college and beyond, are preternaturally self-motivated and almost always have solid, consistent, competent support from their parents. All else being equal, boys and girls from intact, two-parent families tend to do better—not just in school but in all walks of life.

There is a temptation, then, to prescribe marriage as the cure for Abandoned black America's parlous condition. I believe that's unrealistic. By all means, let marriage be a theme hammered home by every preacher, in every pulpit, on every Sunday. But the decline of marriage and the rise of single-parent households are society-wide phenomena, albeit with their greatest impact among African Americans. "Too bad your father's not around" is not a policy prescription; it's a cruel taunt directed at children who are already being victimized by forces beyond their control.

Despite dropout rates of up to 50 percent in some cities, most youths in Abandoned communities do manage to graduate high school. For those who don't, the information age economy has nothing to offer—you can't go down to the plant and sign up for a steady, blue-collar, union job with decent benefits, since the plant was shuttered years ago when this country stopped making things. If you're a young man and you drop out, you spend your days hanging out on the corner; your choice is validated and reinforced by neighborhood friends who took the same route. If you're a young woman and you drop out, you probably get pregnant and have a child; you want the very best for your baby, like every mother does, but you have no real idea how to provide it. Those who stay in school and graduate end up with diplomas that are devalued—and with basic skills that qualify them only for episodic, dead-end employment.

If you are a male dropout and you spend a significant amount of your time with like-minded acquaintances on the corner, there is an excellent chance that you will have opportunities to participate in the illegal economy—the drug trade. Whether you participate or not, being in proximity to the drug business when the police come around is enough to put you in contact with the criminal justice system. Out of 1.5 million prisoners incarcerated in the federal and state prison systems in 2008, an estimated 528,000 were black.[13] The fact that the "statistic" about there being more black men in prison than in college is false gives only cold comfort, because it is indisputably true that the rate of incarceration for African American men—down substantially since the turn of the new century—is still more than twice the rate for Hispanic men and about six times the rate for white men.

Is this somehow intentional? Is the system rigged to warehouse black men in prison? I would argue that mandatory sentencing laws and the differential treatment of offenses involving crack cocaine versus powder cocaine boost the African American incarceration rate, as does the fact that Abandoned black neighborhoods are generally policed with Fort Apache–style aggressiveness. But I don't believe these factors are enough to explain the entire disparity. Family breakdown, untutored parenting, failed schools—all the factors that go into creating and perpetuating Abandoned black America have to be invoked to fully explain why our jails and prisons are full of black men for whom incarceration is almost a rite of passage. The impact is more easily defined than the cause: Ex-offenders have even less chance than non-offenders of ever finding the elusive path that leads to the Mainstream.

And it is in Abandoned neighborhoods where the epidemic of violent crime still rages. The most critical problem was always black-on-black crime, not black-on-white; but it was only when whites and Mainstream blacks felt vulnerable that crime became a hotly debated political issue. Now, for most Americans, crime is distant and much less threatening. For Abandoned black Americans, however, crime is a fact of everyday life. One of the most disheartening developments of the past decade has been the establishment of standard rituals with which to mark the violent taking of a young life—among them, memorial T-shirts with a computer-silk-screened picture of the deceased, along with his or her dates of birth and death. In Washington, such occasions are common enough to make T-shirt shops among the most successful types of businesses in Abandoned black neighborhoods. Along with funeral homes, of course.

* * *

Movie critics loved the 2009 indie film *Precious.* African Americans, not so much.

I shouldn't generalize. The truth is that *Precious* divided black Americans—and divided us passionately—along what by now are familiar aesthetic and cultural lines. There were those who celebrated the skill and artistry of director Lee Daniels, the powerful and unforgettable performances by Mo'Nique and ingenue Gabourey Sidibe, and even the brave choice by Mariah Carey, a diva's diva, to appear on-screen in unflattering makeup that included the subtlest hint of a mustache. With entertainment moguls Oprah Winfrey and Tyler Perry on board as executive producers—basically providing their imprimatur and their money—a film by and about black people had elbowed its way into Hollywood, the ultimate gated community, and taken the place by storm. Not only was the film wildly profitable, given its small budget, but it was in every sense excellent when judged by Hollywood's standards of excellence. *Precious* was acclaimed as a great piece of cinema—which is, by definition, a grand illusion. It wasn't meant to be a documentary. It was art and demanded to be seen and evaluated as art.

Then there were those who said: Sure, right, most of that may be true. The acting was good, depending on how thoroughly you like your scenery chewed, and young Sidibe was truly amazing. But *Precious* wasn't art, it was a form of pornography.

Precious: Based on the Novel Push *by Sapphire* is set in a specific milieu: the Abandoned black America of the nation's most lurid imagination. The story line, said the film's vocal critics, appears to have no more elevated purpose than the arousal of prurient interest: An obese, functionally illiterate teenager is raped and impregnated by her father—not once, but twice. The child born of the first impregnation has Down syndrome. Meanwhile, the girl is also being horribly abused, both physically and psychologically, by her mother, who is evidently one of the most evil and worthless individuals ever to walk the earth. The mother—also obese, incidentally—is the Angry Black Woman from Hell. She sees her daughter not as the pathetic victim she really is but as a rival for the affections of the violent, irredeemable monster—the Worthless Black Man from Hell—who so brutally rapes his own daughter.

"It wasn't until I was at Sundance and this Chinese lady in her 60s started crying in my arms . . . did I realize this was a universal story. That was an epiphany," director Daniels said in a published interview.[14]

Universal? Really? The thing is, this tale of unimaginable horror, cruelty, ignorance, and dysfunction was not imagined to have taken place in San Francisco's Chinatown, the barrios of East Los Angeles, the WASPish Connecticut suburbs, the hills and hollows of Appalachia, the ranchlands of Texas, or any of a million other possible "universal" settings. These desperate creatures were poor and black, and to many people that seemed a striking coincidence. For there were remarkable echoes of a similar tale of incest, abuse, and depravity: *The Color Purple*, another critically acclaimed chronicle of woe set in the black underclass. In the case of Alice Walker's novel, it was the black underclass of the 1930s. Apparently, some things never change.

Interestingly, Winfrey was another thread connecting the two projects: She gave an Oscar-nominated performance in *The Color Purple* and later bankrolled a grand-scale adaptation of the work for the Broadway stage, years before she loaned her name—and brought much of her vast audience—to *Precious*. When asked what drew her to Daniels's film, Winfrey told an interviewer that the protagonist reminded her of anonymous girls she would see on city streets through the window of her limousine—girls whose lives were "invisible" to her.

Winfrey has the standing to make such an observation (to my ear, terribly off-key), having bootstrapped her way from poverty and abuse to unimaginable heights—all the way from Abandoned to Transcendent. But still: What is it with the idea that black plus poor equals not just privation, not just dysfunction, but a pattern of behavior that can only be described as subhuman? What is it that audiences find so compelling about Grand Guignol depictions of African American poverty? Is some urge being satisfied, some itch being scratched? Is some preconceived notion being confirmed?

Or is guilt being assuaged? Is society saying, in effect: Yes, we have turned our backs. Yes, we have left you adrift, knowing that many of you will drown. But look how you behave. Look how you really are. *You deserve it.*

6

THE TRANSCENDENT: WHERE NONE HAVE GONE BEFORE

I n July 2009, President Barack Obama made the short trip to New York City to address the one-hundredth annual convention of the National Association for the Advancement of Colored People. The centennial of the NAACP, the nation's largest and most important civil rights organization, was an obvious occasion for our first African American president to talk about race. Aware of my interest in the theme and the occasion, the White House press office arranged for me to interview the president at the Hilton in midtown right before he delivered his speech. I was on the train heading to New York when I got word that the interview had to be rescheduled— my fifteen-minute window had been slammed shut by more pressing obligations. Instead, I would be able to see the president the following afternoon at the White House.

I reported to the White House at the appointed hour, was buzzed through to the West Wing, and settled in to chat with my handlers; the president was running a few minutes late, dealing with one of the many cliff's-edge crises that his health-care reform initiative had to survive. Finally I was led through a maze of offices and antechambers to the inner sanctum. Obama greeted me at the door to the Oval Office. I sat down on one of the couches, looked around the most famous workspace in the world, and had to take a couple of deep breaths before I could ask my first question. My profession requires cultivating a certain seen-it-all air, but I was pretty overwhelmed.

I got what I needed from the interview, and there were only two other moments when I had to pause for oxygen. The first was when I noticed a bust of the Reverend Martin Luther King Jr. on a sideboard and realized that when Obama sat at his desk, making decisions that would touch all our lives, the bust would be in his direct line of sight. The second was when I noticed who else was in the room: top presidential adviser Valerie Jarrett; her chief of staff, Michael Strautmanis; a press-office liaison, Corey Ealons; and the president of the United States. Everyone in the Oval Office at that moment, including the most powerful man in the world, was African American.

Obama's presidency definitively settles any question of whether a Transcendent black American elite has arisen—a small but growing cohort with the kind of power, wealth, and influence that previous generations of African Americans could never have imagined. Even the last stubborn skeptics must now admit that the Transcendents have arrived.

By skeptics, I refer to the Transcendents themselves. Their dazzling success hides a mountain of self-doubt that now, post-Obama, may finally be eroding.

The president was already Transcendent long before he moved his family into the White House. Being one of just three African Americans ever elected to the Senate is more than enough to qualify. What I found fascinating was how many of his fellow Transcendents were not just unsupportive of his "premature" or even "presumptuous" run for the presidency but actively hostile to it. The first black president began his campaign over the opposition of most of the black political and economic establishment.

The most Transcendent black American of all—pre-Obama, that is—was a notable exception. Oprah Winfrey, whose fortune *Forbes* has estimated at more than $2 billion, presides over a vast entertainment and lifestyle empire whose centerpiece had long been her eponymous syndicated talk show, watched by between six million and seven million viewers every day. With her show, her magazine, and her other ventures, she had earned political capital over the years and kept it like a hoarder, holding tight to every little scrap and shred. Now she decided to spend it on Obama, a fellow Chicagoan whom she knew well. Entertainers, like politicians, succeed wildly when they can see or feel where the culture is headed before anyone else. That doesn't mean that Hollywood is an unerring guide to where the country is headed. But Winfrey had already accomplished the improbable feat that Obama would have to pull off, which was to convince white Americans that she understood their lives and had their interests and well-being not just in her mind but in her heart. It might have been a long shot for an African American to win America's position of highest trust, but she knew it wasn't impossible.

In December 2007, her Oprahpalooza campaign events in Iowa, New Hampshire, and South Carolina gave Obama a big, timely boost in those early-primary states. Even for a tastemaker who routinely plucks unheralded books—and their uncelebrated authors—out of obscurity and vaults them to the top of the best-seller lists, convincing an audience to support a presidential candidate is a challenge of a different order. But my reading of the way the primary campaign played out is that Winfrey not only conveyed to Obama her maximum-wattage star power but also effectively gave some wavering voters permission to take a leap of faith.

I spent most of the week between Christmas and New Year's in Iowa, crisscrossing the frozen state to get a look at the Obama, Hillary Clinton, and John Edwards campaigns in person. I got the clear impression that Winfrey's blessing had soothed the angst that some women I met at Obama rallies felt about forsaking Clinton, the first woman with a realistic chance of becoming president. I don't want to overstate the Oprah effect; a whole host of stars had to align, and in precisely the right order, for an African American freshman senator, with a name that could have come from the Guantánamo inmate rolls, to defeat the most experienced and powerful political machine in the Democratic Party. We'll never know what would have happened if Winfrey had come out as strongly for Clinton as she did for Obama—but it's hard for me to imagine that history would have played out exactly the same.

Other Transcendents in the entertainment world, perhaps blessed with some of Winfrey's foresight or her willingness to embrace the new, also flocked to the charismatic young senator. Among them were Will Smith, who reigned as Hollywood's undisputed king—the most bankable star in town, with an unsurpassed ability to "open" a big-budget movie with huge first-weekend box-office revenue—and his wife, Jada Pinkett Smith, a star in her own right. But in realms such as sports, business, and especially politics, many Transcendent black Americans were surprisingly cool, if not just plain cold, to the first black presidential candidate who was running not to make a point or gain a measure of influence but to win.

Earvin "Magic" Johnson, whose fortune has been estimated at $500 million, recorded a radio ad for the South Carolina primary in which he said he was supporting Clinton because she was the more "prepared and experienced" candidate. He suggested that Obama should heed the advice that a Lakers veteran gave Johnson during his first year as a pro: "Take it easy rookie, it's a long season, it's a long road to the championship."[1] Even by the standards of modern political advertising, this was just dumb. Anyone who had followed Johnson's stellar career knew that in his rookie season, *he led the Lakers to the NBA championship*. It is hard to think of anyone, and I mean anyone in the world, with less standing to tell Obama the "rookie" to be mindful of his place.

Tycoon Robert L. Johnson, who had founded Black Entertainment Television and sold it to Viacom for a reported $3 billion, also had an eruption in the days before the South Carolina primary—the first contest in which substantial numbers of African Americans would vote. Campaigning in Columbia with Clinton, Johnson said that "to me, as an African-American, I am frankly insulted that the Obama campaign would imply that we are so stupid that we would think Hillary and Bill Clinton, who have been deeply and emotionally involved in black issues since Barack Obama was doing something in the neighborhood—and I won't say what he was doing, but he said it in the book—when they have been involved." Referring to Obama's campaign tactics, he added, "That kind of campaign behavior does not resonate with me, for a guy who says, 'I want to be a reasonable, likable, Sidney Poitier *Guess Who's Coming to Dinner*.' And I'm thinking, I'm thinking to myself, this ain't a movie, Sidney. This is real life."[2]

When you untangle the gnarled syntax, Johnson was extolling the Clintons' advocacy on behalf of African American interests over the decades; taking a gratuitous swipe at Obama for the youthful experimentation with illegal drugs that he described in his memoir; and declaring that Obama's candidacy was nothing but a feel-good Hollywood movie with no relationship to "real life." (Bill Clinton sounded the same theme, calling Obama's presidential bid a "fairy tale.")

Andrew Young, an icon of the civil rights movement, joked that Bill Clinton "is every bit as black as Barack" and added that "he's probably gone with more black women than Barack."[3] Other aging luminaries had the good sense not to try stand-up comedy, but the position of the African American political establishment was decidedly pro-Clinton and anti-Obama. Congressman John Lewis of Georgia, who still bears the scars from being savagely beaten on one of the Selma-to-Montgomery marches, supported Clinton, as did a majority of his colleagues in the Congressional Black Caucus. Uberlawyer Vernon Jordan, of course, was solidly in the Clintons' corner; he told friends that African Americans had urgent work to do and didn't have time to waste on "fantasies."

This was the most common theme struck by Transcendent black Americans who did not believe in Obama's candidacy. Some cynics chalked up this attitude to pure calculation: deals made with the Clintons, repayment for old favors, perhaps the fear of losing influence if Clinton didn't win. But I never thought it was that simple. The complaint from Transcendent African Americans was that the whole Obama thing was a beautiful dream, a wonderful fantasy, an inspirational wish— but nothing more. For these Transcendents, it came down to a single question that answered itself: *Do you really think this black man is going to be president? Let's be real.*

This Transcendent skepticism was different from the fatalism I often heard during the campaign from other African Americans—Mainstream and Abandoned—who believed that in the final analysis "they" would never let a black man into the White House, "they" being the white power structure, or the unreformed racists who operate beneath society's radar, or the corporate interests that always seem to get their way. The Transcendents were neither naïve nor paranoid. Those who doubted not just the likelihood but even the possibility of Obama knew that barriers could be broken because they had broken them. Perhaps they knew better than anyone how difficult those breakthroughs had been, and simply could not imagine that this final, ultimate barrier would fall so easily, without a long and bitter siege.

In part, what we saw and heard reflected a generational divide. The elders—those who had lived through the civil rights struggle, like Lewis and Jordan—had an especially difficult time getting their minds around the Obama phenomenon. They knew from experience that the way African Americans got attention and redress at the highest levels of American politics and government was by working with and through sympathetic white politicians. The Clintons were the gold standard in this regard, as evidenced by Toni Morrison's famous quip about Bill Clinton being the first black president. The Republican Party, at the moment, wasn't even making an effort to speak to African Americans. This meant that the Democrats were the only game in town, and with the popularity of the Republican incumbent, George W. Bush, having plunged to subterranean levels, the presidency and increased majorities in both houses of Congress were all but in the bag. In Hillary Clinton, African Americans would have a sympathetic ear and an effective advocate. To veterans of a lifetime of struggle, risking so much on a proposition that could charitably be described as iffy—that white Americans would actually elect a black man president—seemed insane.

More than length of experience alone was at play, however. The first Transcendent black Americans—Vernon Jordan's generation, men and women now mostly in their sixties and seventies—successfully forced, cajoled, wheedled, or otherwise inserted themselves into places where they did not belong. Their achievement overcame, but did not erase, the fact that their exalted status was unauthorized, and thus precarious. All the confidence and smooth bluster in the world couldn't change that—and all of the comforts, privileges, and prerogatives in the world were not enough, for some Transcendents, to foster a proper sense of entitlement. In the luxurious but not entirely serene precincts of Transcendent black America, Hillary Clinton was the smart, conservative play, the best that could be hoped for. Only those foolish enough not to steal nervous glances over their shoulders were able to look at the field and conclude that yes, Obama could.

* * *

There have been Transcendent black Americans since before black Americans were free. Until quite recently, however, there were never more than a handful at a time.

Frederick Douglass, born a slave, was one of the nation's best-known and most influential abolitionists, a statesman whose counsel was valued by President Lincoln. During Reconstruction, the first African Americans were elected to Congress. Around the turn of the century, Booker T. Washington was known across the country as a leader of, and spokes-man for, black Americans—his fame, at least in the South, due in no small part to his prescription of slow, don't-rock-the-boat progress that did not involve a demand for integration. W. E. B. DuBois, during this same period, was recognized as a towering intellectual and a fiery activist. Joe Louis ruled as heavyweight champion of the world, the first of a succession of African American boxers whose skill elevated them to the Transcendent realm. Toward midcentury, African Americans like Ralph Bunche, the diplomat who served as principal secretary of the United Nations and received the 1950 Nobel Peace Prize, and the most prominent musicians and athletes—Duke Ellington, Miles Davis, Jackie Robinson, Jim Brown—had Transcendent status, as did Roy Wilkins when he headed the NAACP and, of course, the young Dr. King in his prime.

But these luminaries of the past were isolated individu-als, and their wealth, power, and influence were relative. An example would be John H. Johnson, the grandson of slaves, who created a publishing empire in Chicago. Johnson's mag-azines, *Ebony* and *Jet*, were enormously important to African Americans and thoroughly saturated their marketplace; when I was young, it was rare to go into a black household and not see at least one of the two magazines lying around somewhere. Johnson's publications were brave and authoritative in cov-ering civil rights, and in an important way they helped knit pre-disintegration black America together. But Johnson had no peer group of black media barons—there was no black William Randolph Hearst or Joseph Pulitzer to complement his version of Henry Luce. And while Johnson was virtually a monopolist, the market he owned consisted exclusively of African Ameri-cans. At my house, we subscribed to Luce's iconic titles—*Time* and *Life*—as well as Johnson's. But are there *any* white Americans my age who grew up with *Ebony* or *Jet* on the coffee table?

Now, for the first time, there is a large enough cohort of Transcendent black Americans to form a critical mass. This group is wealthy, powerful, and influential not just in comparison to other African Americans but in absolute terms.

This meant that the first African American president, confronting the direst financial crisis since the Great Depression, was able to summon an experienced African American CEO (Richard Parsons) out of retirement to oversee troubled Citigroup. It meant that when the president went to work on his campaign promise to bring the treatment of terrorism suspects back into line with civilized norms, he could task an African American attorney general (Eric Holder) with the job. It meant that as President Obama decided on diplomatic steps he could take to rid the United States of its Crazy Cowboy image in the world and chart a new course, he could pick up the phone and call *two* African American former secretaries of state (Colin Powell and Condoleezza Rice) for advice—although the president had to keep in mind that one of them had been the Chief Cowgirl.

The critical mass that makes Transcendent black America real and important is a direct consequence of the successes of the 1960s—civil rights, desegregation, affirmative action, black political empowerment. These achievements pushed open long-sealed doors, just a crack, and exceptional individuals bulled their way through. It was a natural process: First a few individuals managed to poke their heads above the Mainstream, and then a few more, and eventually there were enough to have real impact—not just on black America but on the nation and the world.

I watched the process happen. I was hired by *The Washington Post* in 1980 to cover the city's charismatic mayor Marion Barry during his first term. This was long before Barry's crack-smoking downfall and eventual semi-redemption. He had been elected with the support of constituencies that eventually became disillusioned and bitter foes—liberal whites, the growing gay population, young and highly educated black professionals, the editorial board of the *Post*—and he promised new competence and efficiency.

And believe it or not, he delivered: Under Barry, the city government had the first clean audit of its finances and floated its first bond issue. This was a big step, since the books had been such a mess, and to get it done Barry hired the investment bank Lazard Freres. The adviser that Lazard sent was a razor-sharp young black man named Franklin Raines—the same man who, nearly three decades later, would be accused of helping create the subprime mortgage mess as the Transcendent chairman and CEO of Fannie Mae.

When I met him, Raines was in his early thirties. Born in Seattle, he had humble, working-class origins; his father was a janitor. I remember a story he told me at the time: His mother had decided that he would be called "Frank Delno Raines" in honor of family members with those names. But when she wrote that down at the hospital, a white clerk assumed that she was an ignorant black woman who didn't know how to spell the name of the thirty-second president properly. The baby's name was recorded as "Franklin Delano Raines" instead.

Raines was born in 1949. Had he been born in, say, 1929, he still would certainly have been a success—he's too smart and driven not to have made a mark. But his life surely would have been different.

Two decades earlier, it would have been much less likely for even a young black man as bright as Raines to attend Harvard College—black students didn't arrive on Ivy League campuses in substantial numbers until the late 1960s. It would have been unlikely for him to study at Oxford's Magdalen College as a Rhodes scholar, since there were no black American Rhodes Scholars for five decades, between in 1907 and 1963. It's highly unlikely that he would have been able to graduate from Harvard Law.

Raines got his credentials just in time to join the first sizable group of black professionals who were allowed to climb the well-trod ladder that zigzags between government and high finance. He started in the Carter administration, then took refuge at Lazard, then was recruited through his Democratic Party connections to jump to Fannie Mae, then was lured back into government under the Clinton administration as director of the Office of Management and Budget—one of the most powerful jobs in a city that worships power the way other cities worship money—and then finally went back to Fannie Mae in 1999 as the first black CEO of a Fortune 500 company. Other African Americans would soon follow him in that distinction—Kenneth Chenault at American Express, Stanley O'Neal at Merrill Lynch—but Raines was the one who planted the flag.

The Fannie Mae job did not end well. In December 2004, Raines took what he called "early retirement" after Fannie Mae was accused of overstating its profits over several years by more than $6 billion. Four years later, Fannie Mae's aggressive expansion on Raines's watch was blamed as a major cause of the subprime mortgage meltdown. O'Neal, too, was cited for his role in the financial collapse—of all the large invest-

ment banks, Merrill had made the biggest and most irresponsible bet on subprimes. It was a milestone, albeit not one that
would be universally celebrated: For the first time, two African
Americans had become big enough players in the financial
world to have major roles—I should say allegedly—in trigger-
ing a global economic crisis. Genuine entitlement includes the
privilege to fail.

Another Marion Barry initiative was to bring the new technology called cable television to the District of Columbia. This
required awarding a lucrative contract for cable service in
the city, and groups of well-connected insiders were formed
to compete for the concession. Most big-city African American mayors have tried to foster African American economic
development through the awarding of municipal contracts
and concessions; few have done this as effectively as Barry.
When he took office, Washington's business community was
old, white, established, clubby, and complacent. Barry used
his power over city contracts to create a new class of millionaire black developers, lawyers, and consultants. Among them
was Robert Johnson.

Johnson was born in Mississippi in 1946—the ninth of ten
children—and grew up mostly in Illinois, graduating from
the University of Illinois and later earning a master's degree
from Princeton University's Woodrow Wilson School of Public and International Affairs. While Raines bounced back and
forth between money and politics, Johnson went straight for
the intersection of the two: lobbying. More specifically, he
worked for the National Cable & Telecommunications Association, where he gained the knowledge and contacts that he
would eventually put to spectacularly lucrative use. Like all
great salesmen, he is unnaturally persistent and persuasive.

And like few human beings I've ever met, he has an amazing ability to quickly and effortlessly manipulate numbers in his head.

When I first met him in 1980, Johnson was a smart young entrepreneur hanging around the mayor's office and the press room, trying to land a contract that would make his company Washington's first cable-television provider. He had no chance—other groups bidding on the lucrative contract had better connections and more juice—but somehow he prevailed. He told anyone who would listen that the cable franchise would be just a start, that he intended to use it as a launching pad for a national cable network aimed at African American viewers. A colleague of mine in the city hall press corps pulled him aside, with genuine concern, and soberly advised him to forget the Don Quixote routine and get a real job. Fortunately, Johnson ignored him. He and his wife, Sheila, built District Cablevision into BET and BET into an empire, ultimately selling it to Viacom in 2001 for a reported $3 billion.

Johnson lost his billionaire status when he and Sheila divorced in 2002, splitting the fortune into roughly half-billion-dollar chunks. The separation had the effect of making Sheila Johnson a Transcendent figure in her own right. And it was thanks to her that I saw for the first time what Transcendent status looks like in the social world.

Before the split, the Johnsons bought a two-hundred-acre estate near Middleburg in the Virginia hunt country west of Washington. Gatsby-esque doesn't do justice to the night in December 2001 when Sheila, a café-au-lait-skinned woman with a disarmingly sweet smile, hosted a little fund-raiser for her favorite cause: preventing Washington's rapacious suburban sprawl from encroaching on the bucolic Johnson spread, which they had named Salamander Farm. The event took place after Bob had already moved out.

Arriving guests were relieved of their car keys by an army of valet-parking attendants and welcomed into what looked at first like a wing of a great mansion. It turned out, though, that this wasn't the big house, which was out of sight on the other side of a hill. We were being herded into the stables, which had stalls made of a wood that looked like cherry. An antique clock hung on the wall. The stalls were occupied, and fellow guests who knew about such things pronounced the horses magnificent.

The stables led to an indoor equestrian ring that the Johnsons had built for their daughter, Paige, a talented rider who had her eye on the Olympics. What should have been a muddy, smelly place had been transformed for the evening. At the door, each guest was dusted with an individual sprinkling of artificial snow—a way of announcing the "winter wonderland" theme. Each table had an elaborate, towering centerpiece that looked like a bare branch of a snowbound tree. A performance stage had been erected and an enormous dance floor laid: the entertainment was Ashford and Simpson, complete with their full band, sound and lighting technicians, the works. We had reached the day when a black woman could throw the biggest, flashiest party of the year in a town of millionaires.

A few years later, Sheila Johnson was an early believer in the proposition that we had reached the day when a black man could be elected president. But many of her fellow Transcendents vehemently disagreed.

Bob Johnson, as we've seen, scoffed at the early rumors of an Obama candidacy and told friends he didn't think the country was "ready" for a black president. Johnson was an old friend of the Clintons, and perhaps that friendship meant there was never any real question of which camp he would join. But I believe there was more to it than that. Ever since I met Johnson all those years ago at the District Building, his business model had always been explicitly race-conscious. He didn't just start a television network; he started a *black* television network. As a CEO, he always kept a sharp eye on the bottom line; one reason BET became so valuable was that it resisted the temptation to produce lots of expensive original programming that the potential audience—limited by the African American focus—might not be able to support. Yet on the frequent occasions when Johnson was criticized by African Americans for the dearth of news and public affairs on BET's schedule, and the lavish overabundance of booty-shaking hip-hop videos, he seemed genuinely hurt. After he sold the network, as his "second act" he established a conglomerate, RLJ Companies, that invested in banking, finance, hotels—an oddly diverse assortment of businesses. I once asked him how he decided where to invest his money, and he answered with a maxim: "I like to look for business sectors where African Americans are not represented, and I go there."

In short, he is what used to be called a "race man"—ever mindful of being African American, of serving African American interests, and of making breakthroughs on behalf of African Americans. It was striking, and on the surface somewhat puzzling, that such a race-conscious man would so ardently oppose the first serious attempt by an African American to win the presidency.

But in a way, that was the point. I dwell on Obama's candidacy because it was such a Rorschach test for the Transcendent class. Bob Johnson's mind-set was broadly representative of those who stuck with the Clintons, in my view, and it was characterized above all by a certain rock-hard wariness. The elder Transcendents were used to surviving in terra incognita. They got where they are by being the "first black" this and the "first black" that, by taking on responsibilities that no African American had ever shouldered before, and by enduring the intense and unrelenting scrutiny that "first black" status always entails. They knew the experience of being the only black person around a boardroom table and always assuming—always knowing, they would say—that all eyes were on the one person who wasn't like the others, who didn't belong. They saw in Obama a man who gave no outward sign of harboring within him that hard nugget of suspicion—who seemed as if he were not artfully concealing the chip on his shoulder but in fact did not have one. They saw a man who seemed to glide through life on a cushion of good fortune. Never mind that this wasn't true, as evidenced by Obama's well-corroborated account of his hardly privileged childhood. Never mind that despite Obama's not having had a "typical" African American upbringing, he had come to fully embrace his identity as African American— witness his marriage to Michelle, his work in Chicago's black community, his membership in Jeremiah Wright's church. Never mind that his tastes and mannerisms were indisputably African American, down to the way he walked. To some Transcendents, he wasn't black enough.

Indeed, soon after Obama announced his candidacy in 2007, the media zeitgeist became briefly preoccupied with that very question—whether Obama was "black enough." It was all the buzz in February when Obama visited my hometown of Orangeburg for a rally. I flew down to cover the event, and it was amusing to watch the reporters from national media outlets fan out into the crowd at Claflin University's Tullis Arena and buttonhole my old friends and neighbors with the "black enough" question. From Mainstream black Americans, I never heard concern or even speculation about the degree of Obama's blackness. Yes, he was biracial—but anyone could see that he was black. Case closed. Plus, he was married to a black woman who radiated black pride, even without saying a word. Case definitively closed. I never heard the "black enough" question from Abandoned black Americans, either. All you had to do was look at him. What else was he going to be?

From a few Transcendents, however, I did hear that question. They phrased it differently, though. They asked about his political history, his relationship with the African American leadership, his air of calm and reserve. They observed the "post-racial" tone of his campaign—basically, don't talk about race unless an uproar over Reverend Wright forces you to—and while they understood that this approach was politically necessary, they were unsettled. Transcendents I talked to worried that in all the ways that Bob Johnson is a "race man," Barack Obama isn't.

They worried that he was naïve about the power of race in American society. They worried that if he somehow managed to win the nomination, he would surely lose a general election that Clinton probably would have won—which would mean at least four more years in which issues vital to black Americans were ignored. A couple of people I talked to even looked ahead to a possible Obama victory, and worried that as the first black president, he would have to bend over backward to avoid being seen as favoring African Americans—which could mean less attention to the plight of Abandoned black Americans than under a Clinton administration. They worried that the question that had driven and guided black leadership for more than a century—What is best for the race?—was not central enough for Obama. It wasn't that Obama's Transcendent black critics believed he was indifferent to the needs of African Americans, or that they believed Hillary Clinton was somehow more of a "race man" than Obama was. It was more that they saw the whole Obama phenomenon as a self-indulgent fantasy—one for which black Americans had no time, and for which these Transcendents had no patience.

With rare exceptions, Transcendents who are old enough to have lived through segregation don't just remember the experience but cling to it. They use it to give them motivation, to inspire caution, to remind them how hard-won their success was and how radically the world can change within a human lifetime. Anyone who lived through Jim Crow knows firsthand that other people can reject you, even despise you, based on nothing but the color of your skin. This knowledge can be crippling, even paralyzing, or it can provide a reservoir of strength and defiance. But with that strength comes an indelible wariness and the knowledge that however meaningless race might be, it does matter.

The Obamas know that, too. But they have been clever enough to "code" their major initiatives in such a way that they are designed to provide sorely needed benefits to African American and other disadvantaged communities—without explicitly being aimed at any one group.

Michelle Obama's most high-profile cause, fighting childhood obesity, is a case in point. The problem is serious among all segments of American society, as a walk through any shopping mall will demonstrate. Among whites, about 31 percent of children are obese. But among African American children, the obesity rate is 35 percent; and among the children of Mexican Americans, an alarming 38 percent.[4] Any success the First Lady's campaign has will be beneficial to the health and well-being of all the nation's children, but the need is more acute—and the impact will be greater—among minorities.

Likewise, President Obama's signature legislative accomplishment, won at the price of tons of his political capital, will also disproportionately benefit minorities. About 18 percent of black Americans lack health insurance, and while that figure is only marginally higher than the 16 percent of whites who are uninsured, the gap among black children and white children is greater. Among Latino Americans, a striking 33 percent are without insurance.[5] Race-neutral policies, it turns out, do not always have race-neutral impacts.

* * *

One of my favorite episodes of the long campaign, at least in terms of entertainment value, occurred in February 2008 after reporters noticed that parts of an Obama speech were strikingly similar to passages of a speech given by one of his campaign chairmen. On Fox News, commentator Geraldo Rivera sputtered with outrage through his famous mustache: "When I saw that they were the same words that Deval Patrick, the black guy who won as Massachusetts mayor—as Massachusetts governor—had used, I said to myself, it seems so premeditated. It's almost as if they went to a camp where these black geniuses got together and figured out how to beat the political system . . . What's the other formula that they're going to use?"[6]

"Black Genius Camp" was a delightful image to play with—
you could imagine Denzel Washington and Maya Angelou sitting around the campfire, listening to Condi Rice tell corny
jokes in Russian. But there was actually a germ of truth in what
Rivera said.

Obama represents a next-generation cohort of black political and economic leaders whose experience of being black in
America is radically different from that of their elders. In that
Oval Office interview after his NAACP speech, Obama told me:
"If we haven't already reached this point we're getting close to
reaching it, where there are going to be more African Americans in this country who never experienced anything remotely
close to Jim Crow than those who lived under Jim Crow. That,
obviously, changes perspectives."[7]

That change is especially pertinent when the perspectives
in question are those of African Americans with Transcendent
power, influence, or wealth. In the political realm, this younger
group includes Deval Patrick, the first black governor of Massachusetts and only the second African American elected governor of any state (after Virginia's Douglas Wilder); Newark
mayor Cory Booker; D.C. mayor Adrian Fenty; Alabama congressman Artur Davis; and a host of other rising young officeholders, or aspiring officeholders, around the country. There
is no evidence that they actually attended a genius camp
together, but there are so many connections among them that
they do constitute a network. They tend to have attended the
same elite schools, and they have been instrumental in getting
one another elected. They are surrounded and supported by
a much larger group of black professionals—the friends from
college or law school who decided not to go into politics and

instead became partners in big law firms or rose through the ranks in the corporate world.

These young Transcendents, generally in their forties, are indeed too young to have lived through Jim Crow. They are not too young to know what it was, and certainly not too young to believe as passionately as their elders in the need to keep fighting to advance the unfinished project of black uplift. But there is a difference between knowing what it is like to face racism and discrimination, which this next-generation black elite does, and knowing what it is like to be consigned by law and police authority to second-class citizenship, which it does not. In that sense, the post-segregation Transcendents carry less baggage through life.

And perhaps, having just missed the epochal civil rights triumph, this generation of Transcendents feels it has something to prove—that it is time for the aging lions of the civil rights struggle to step aside, and that new strategies and tactics are required for a new era.

It is also true, however, that for some young Transcendents, maintaining or developing any sort of common touch is a challenge. A case in point is Harold Ford Jr., the former Tennessee congressman who is one of the best and brightest of his generation. The scion of the most powerful black family in Tennessee politics, Ford was born in 1970 and grew up mostly in Washington while his father served in Congress. He graduated from St. Albans, the most prestigious boys' prep school in the capital, and went on to the University of Pennsylvania and the University of Michigan Law School before winning the congressional seat his father had long held.[8] Political handicappers saw Ford as handsome, charming, and bright enough to be a kind of Southern-fried Obama. In 2006, Ford came close to duplicating Obama's feat and winning a seat in the U.S. Senate. He ran in his home state of Tennessee, and the contest became infamous because of a last-minute attack ad by his opponent that had clear racial overtones: It ended with a ditzy-seeming blonde pantomiming a telephone and asking Ford to "call me," and seemed designed to stoke the primal Southern fear of black men consorting with white women. Dispassionate analysis of the election returns suggest, however, that Ford probably would have lost even if the ad had never aired.

Ford moved to New York and joined Merrill Lynch as a senior adviser—a "rainmaker," basically. He prepared to run for the Senate again, but this time from New York, where being labeled a "carpetbagger" is hardly the kiss of death—witness Hillary Clinton's election as a senator from New York, and Robert Kennedy's before her. Ford seemed to be well-positioned, but then he gave what came to be seen as a disastrous interview to *The New York Times* in which he talked about his life as a New Yorker—but not a regular New Yorker, a Master of the Universe New Yorker. He mentioned a flight he had taken to Palm Beach. He disclosed that he had only visited Staten Island once, and that was by helicopter. He let slip that he has breakfast most mornings at the Regency Hotel, which is on Park Avenue. And, as a kind of coup de grace, he revealed that he gets frequent pedicures.[9]

Ford soon announced that he would not be running for the New York Senate seat after all. It is a measure of how far we've come that an African American man has breakfast at the Regency and a regular pedicure appointment—and that, like so many privileged white politicians before him, he can be so tone-deaf.

When I asked Obama about generational succession and its impact on African Americans, this is what he said:

"I think now young people growing up realize, you know what, being African American can mean a whole range of things. There's a whole bunch of possibilities out there for how you want to live your life, what values you want to express, who you choose to interact with. I would say that the downside of this is you don't have the same unifying experience, even though it was a negative experience, of discrimination that let people, at least in the early '60s, all to be on the same page, or to be largely on the same page in terms of how to make progress as a group.

"And I do think it is important for the African American community, in its diversity, to stay true to one core aspect of the African American experience, which is we know what it's like to be on the outside, we know what it's like to be discriminated against, or at least to have family members who have been discriminated against. And if we ever lose that, then I think we're in trouble. Then I think we've lost our way."

Coming from almost anyone else, that would make perfect sense. But it rings somewhat false to hear the president of the United States—the ultimate insider—talk about staying true to the feeling of being "on the outside." Obama lays out the essential contradiction that Transcendent black Americans struggle constantly to resolve: not being outside anymore. For the younger Transcendents, this means holding on to experiences they never actually had—not an act of remembering but of imagining.

7

THE EMERGENT (PART 1): COMING TO AMERICA

In May 2009, Bemnet Faris, a junior at Albert Einstein High School in Maryland, wrote a letter to President Obama. Her hope was "to illuminate the massive economic, political, and social chaos the Ethiopian dictator Prime Minister Meles Zenawi is inflicting on the innocent Ethiopian people." Bemnet wrote that she feared Meles Zenawi was leading the nation "into complete anarchy and an inevitable genocide." The letter went on to describe the situation in Ethiopia in specific and exhaustive detail, highlighting opponents of the regime who had been jailed or killed and building a strong case against Meles Zenawi's rule. In the name of human rights and regional stability, Bemnet argued for action by the U.S. president. Her manifesto read as if it had been written by an exiled Ethiopian scholar or opposition leader, or perhaps a think tank's resident expert on the region. Coming from a high-school student, it was remarkable—even from a girl who has an unblemished record of straight A's, hopes to go to Harvard, and intends to become a pediatric neurosurgeon.

I came to read this letter because Bemnet's father handed me a copy in exchange for a used towel.

At that time, Bemnet's proud papa, Sentayu, was the locker-room attendant at the gym where I exercise. He picked up the dirty laundry, cleaned the sinks, made sure there was enough soap and toilet paper. His English was rudimentary, heavily accented, and somewhat improvisational, which is one reason why few of the members even tried to converse with him beyond "Good morning." Many didn't seem to notice him at all. Sentayu was, for all intents and purposes, invisible.

But his daughter won't be.

With little fanfare, the United States is experiencing the biggest wave of black immigration the nation has seen since the importation of slaves was outlawed in 1808. These newcomers from Africa and the Caribbean constitute one of two distinct segments of an Emergent black America that is beginning to challenge traditional notions of what being "black" even means.

According to the Census Bureau, about 8 percent of U.S. citizens and legal residents who identify themselves as black are foreign-born—roughly one out of twelve. This figure is somewhat misleading, however, because it masks the fact that black immigration is a regional phenomenon. In much of the South, which is still home to the majority of African Americans, black immigration is negligible; not even 1 percent of black people in Mississippi, Alabama, Louisiana, South Carolina, or Arkansas are foreign-born. But in the states where African and Caribbean immigrants do settle—and where black people are a smaller percentage of the overall population—the numbers give a different sense of the newcomers' impact. In New York, Massachusetts, and Minnesota, one of every four black people is foreign-born; in Florida and Washington State, it's one of every five.[1]

Well over half of these new black Americans come from the Caribbean, with the biggest contingents coming from Jamaica, Haiti, and Trinidad, but with all the islands substantially represented. In historical terms, this is no surprise. Caribbean immigrants have long played major roles in black America. Jamaica-born Marcus Garvey, the would-be Moses who tried to lead his people back to Africa, was one of the most prominent and influential black voices of the early part of the twentieth century. Everyone is familiar with the contributions of such second-generation overachievers as Colin Powell, the first black secretary of state, whose parents are from Jamaica, and Eric Holder, the first black attorney general, who is the son of immigrants from Barbados. Going back much further, many thousands of African slaves were "cured" on Caribbean islands—acclimated to the New World environment and "broken" to their new masters' will—before being brought to America to work on the plantations. Oral history in my family says that a distant ancestor arrived, as did many other Africans, via a long-established route from Barbados to the teeming port of Charleston.

What is something of a surprise is the stunning increase in the flow of immigrants from the African continent, with the biggest national groups being Nigerians, Ethiopians, and Ghanaians. These newcomers, many of them as invisible as my friend Sentayu, defy expectations. Here is a supreme historical irony: For nearly two hundred years, Africans were kidnapped, brought here in chains, forced to work without pay, bought and sold like pieces of property, and deliberately kept untutored and illiterate for fear that knowledge would make them uncontrollable and dangerous. Today, Africans coming here voluntarily on wide-body jets are the best-educated immigrants in the United States—better-educated than Asians, Europeans, Latin Americans, or any other regional group.

The Little Ethiopia business district in Washington's U Street corridor is also a Little Eritrea, and the grievances between the two countries, historically one nation, have survived the journey. If you take a taxicab in the capital, see from the ID tag that your driver has a name like Ghebreselassie, and decide to make small talk by saying something nice about Ethiopia, you risk spending the rest of your ride being subjected to a stern lecture—from the Eritrean point of view—about geopolitics on the Horn of Africa.

In most U.S. metropolitan areas, Nigerians constitute by far the biggest national group of African immigrants, which makes sense because Nigeria is by far the most populous nation in black Africa. The cultural norms that dominate in most African immigrant communities are West African. In Washington, uniquely, the Ethiopians and Eritreans predominate. They provide the African immigrant community's flavor and set its Abyssinian tone.

The restaurants, record stores, and other businesses near Howard University are the most visible manifestation of the Ethiopian presence in Washington, but actually the community is widely dispersed, living mostly in the Maryland suburbs of Montgomery and Prince George's counties. Throughout American history, immigrant groups have tended to cluster around particular occupations or industries; once you would find a disproportionate number of Irish police officers, just as now you will find a disproportionate number of Korean dry cleaners. In the Washington area, Ethiopian immigrants have gravitated toward livelihoods involving automobiles.

As anyone who visits the city can see, quite a few are making a living as taxi drivers—one of the quintessential just-off-the-boat jobs. What is not immediately apparent is that D.C. cab companies with names like Action, Alert, Ambassador, and Atlantic—and that's just the A's—are owned by Ethiopian immigrant entrepreneurs.[2] It's no exaggeration to say that Ethiopian immigrants are becoming Washington's taxicab kingpins. As proof, in 2009 two Ethiopian cab-company owners were implicated in a scandal involving alleged kickbacks paid to a city official. Having the juice to be accused of pay-to-play municipal corruption is perhaps the surest sign that an immigrant community has arrived.

Ethiopian immigrants have also moved into the parking industry, although more as employees than employers. Whenever you use one of the city's overpriced lots, it is likely that the gentleman who parks your car and the polite woman who deprives you of your money will have been born in Ethiopia.

Still, taxicabs and parking lots do not leave a particularly large footprint for such a fast-growing, highly educated immigrant group. That imprint is yet to come: It is the children of these African and Caribbean newcomers who, I am confident, will soon make their presence known. I can make that prediction because I know that there is not just one Bemnet Faris. There are many.

My first body of evidence is largely anecdotal but quite voluminous. Several years ago my wife, Avis, started a nonprofit whose mission was to funnel high-achieving African American high-school students from the Washington area into the nation's top-ranked colleges and universities, with all the support and financial aid they needed to succeed. The first step in the process was getting the high schools to identify these students, based on a well-defined set of criteria—grade point average, SAT or ACT scores, letters of recommendation. When the first set of applications started rolling in from students considered by their high-school principals and guidance counselors as the best of the best, nearly 40 percent were from students with surnames like Tsegaye, Olatunde, Arowojolu, Agboke, Getachew, and Diallo—identifiably African names.

This presented an obvious question. The program was clearly a form of affirmative action. But was the purpose of affirmative action to compensate the descendants of people who were enslaved and oppressed? If so, that would exclude the sons and daughters of recent immigrants. Or did affirmative action have the forward-looking purpose of fostering diversity in a society where soon there will be no racial or ethnic majority? If that was the case, then immigrants should be treated like everyone else.

Avis decided, and I concurred, that it would be wrong to try to draw some kind of bright line between students who presumably were the children of immigrants and those who presumably were not. For one thing, presumption is an inexact science; using names as a proxy for country of origin would miss almost all Caribbean immigrants (although you could argue that immigrants from the West Indies shouldn't be excluded in any event, since they, too, were the descendants of slaves). Relying on names as a filter would fail to "catch" some African immigrants as well. And why shouldn't a special exception be made for Liberians, since the country was settled by the descendants of American slaves? But then wouldn't a distinction have to be made between Liberians who were descended from freed American slaves and Liberians who weren't?

Leaving aside the practical question of whether sorting out the immigrants would even be possible, it became obvious that some of the students with African-looking surnames came from extremely low-income households, while some of those with non-African names came from families whose income and net worth made them solidly Mainstream—or, in some cases, just plain affluent. It would not make sense to offer help to the black daughter of a corporate vice president but withhold it from the black son of two parking-lot attendants, no matter where their parents or grandparents were born.

The trend we were seeing was evident around the country, wherever African immigrants had settled in substantial numbers: Their children were performing so well in school that they were overrepresented, relative to their overall numbers, in the lists of overachievers. In 2009, sociologists Pamela R. Bennett of Johns Hopkins University and Amy Lutz of Syracuse University published a paper in the journal *Sociology of Education* that revealed just how well the immigrants were doing. Bennett and Lutz looked at data from the National Education Longitudinal Study of 1988, which follows a large, nationally representative sample of students who were eighth-graders that year. Crunching the numbers, Bennett and Lutz found that black immigrant children—defined as those who were immigrants themselves, or were the children of immigrants—were stellar academic achievers not only when compared to native-born blacks but when compared to whites as well. They reported that 9.2 percent of immigrant black students went on to enroll in elite colleges, such as those in the Ivy League, versus 7.3 percent of whites and 2.4 percent of native blacks. Immigrant black students also had the highest rate of overall college attendance, including non-elite as well as elite schools—75.1 percent of the immigrant blacks enrolled in college, compared to 72.5 percent of whites and 60.2 percent of native blacks.[3]

The sociologists discovered that the immigrant black students were more likely than native black students to come from two-parent households, and that they were also more likely to have attended private high schools—two factors that increase a student's chances of attending an elite college. That finding about two-parent families requires some elaboration. Remember that black immigrant families, particularly those from African countries, are generally not just intact but also highly educated. For a variety of reasons, the parents may not have been able to find jobs in this country that are fully commensurate with their skills; home-country professional qualification in medicine or law, for example, obviously does not allow an immigrant to land at JFK or Dulles one day and start practicing as a doctor or lawyer the next. But even if the father is an accountant who has to work as a security guard while he studies to become certified in this country or the mother is a teacher who is putting food on the table by working as a custodian, the family has a history of education and a reverence for learning. They are likely to know what it takes to guide and motivate a child toward excellence because they will have undergone the process themselves—a process that may involve strict parental discipline, researchers have found, and that may be notably successful in inculcating children against negative peer-group influences. And while each parent may be working long hours to make ends meet, perhaps even holding down two jobs, having both parents in the household means stability and predictability—and creates the expectation that the children will lead stable and predictable lives.

There are also cultural norms that come into play. Not just in Africa but in much of the third world, subjecting the family to shame or disgrace is an awful transgression—if not unthinkable, then certainly unacceptable. Respect for parental authority, and for one's elders in general, is not so much demanded as assumed. Based on evidence that I admit is wholly unscientific and anecdotal, the many African immigrant or first-generation high-school students that I have met in recent years have been adept at walking the tightrope between being "normal" teenagers—loving hip-hop, wearing the right clothes, fitting in—and acceding to heavy-duty academic and social demands at home.

I believe there is an important psychological factor as well. Most immigrants who surmount all the obstacles and make it to the United States are accustomed to success. Whatever degree of political and economic dysfunction their home countries might be suffering, the immigrants managed to master or escape the local context. By virtue of their presence, they are among the winners in their societies. Optimism comes easily, and with it a certain sense of entitlement. All or some of this gets passed down to the next generation.

African and Caribbean immigrants come from societies where there may be ethnic tension but only rarely is there racial tension. The question of whether the black majority would hold political power, and at least share in holding economic power, was decided long ago in source countries such as Nigeria, Ethiopia, and Ghana, and on islands across the Caribbean. In effect, the immigrants are coming from societies that in some ways are similar to the all-black Orangeburg in which my sister and I were raised—not wealthy, to be sure, but proud, economically diverse, and socially integrated.

There is ample evidence that the first-generation, American-born sons and daughters of black immigrants from Africa and the Caribbean perform better in school than their

African American counterparts. Much less clear is what happens to second-generation black immigrants; some studies have found a drop-off, with the overachieving determination and drive of the immigrants having been passed down to their children but not their grandchildren.

A 2007 paper published in *Social Psychology Quarterly* by researchers at the City University of New York and Stanford University suggests that cultural identification might be a factor. The first generation, this argument goes, self-identifies as Jamaican American or Nigerian American, and is largely immune to "stereotype threat"—the phenomenon in which members of a group that is subjected to negative stereotypes perform less well when those stereotypes are made salient. For example, black students will score lower on a standardized test if they are told beforehand that black students do not do well on standardized tests. The researchers from CUNY and Stanford, who used performance on a standardized test as a measure, found that stereotype threat had little or no effect on first-generation Caribbean immigrant students but that it had significant impact on second-generation students—who were more likely to have dropped their country-of-origin identification and begun to consider themselves "black" or "African American."[4] All of which may prove nothing, except that who we are depends on who we *believe* we are.

The Washington-area Ethiopian community, estimated by local activists to number 150,000,[5] has been called the biggest, most affluent, and most important outside of the mother country. Ethiopia's best-known and most highly acclaimed director, Haile Gerima, lives in Washington and teaches film at Howard University. His 1993 movie, *Sankofa*, is a powerful examination of the horrors of slavery; his newest work, *Teza*, is about a fictional Ethiopian intellectual who returns to his homeland during the brutal reign of Mengistu Haile Mariam. The community has an English-Amharic bilingual newspaper, *Zethiopia*, which in July 2009 proudly reported that a local Ethiopian American woman—Mehret Ayalew Mandefro, thirty-two, a Harvard-trained doctor from suburban Alexandria, Virginia—had been named a White House Fellow. Since 1992, the nonprofit Ethiopian Community Center has helped immigrants get settled in their new home, offering classes in English, computer literacy, and other needed skills. Now some of the center's early clients are coming back and asking for help in teaching their Americanized children about the glories of Ethiopian history and culture.

Keeping history alive is important for all early-generation immigrants, but even more important for Ethiopians than most. Ethiopia is believed to have been the birthplace of the human race; some of the very earliest known hominid fossils, dating back 3.2 million years, were found there. More recently, the land once called Abyssinia was one of the great empires of the ancient world, known to the Egyptians, Greeks, Persians, and Romans as an important regional power. Ethiopians were among the leaders in the development of civilization—how we live together, govern ourselves, provide for our basic needs, organize our thinking about life, death, love, family, commerce, community, nation.

Ethiopia also presented humanity with smaller gifts. One of the tasks that Sentayu performed at my gym—before he left for a better-paying job—was to keep the coffee machine in the lounge area functional. When it broke down, which was fairly often, he made coffee at home and brought it to the gym in big thermoses. "Much better," he said proudly of his home brew.

"You know, coffee is from my country. Ethiopia gave coffee to the world!"

He and the other immigrants know who they are and where they come from. The native-born, with a few exceptions, quite literally don't. As the immigrants' numbers and impact grow, I wonder what, if anything, that difference will come to mean.

When our ancestors were brought here, slave owners waged a deliberate, thorough, and successful campaign to erase all traces of our prior cultures. There were, for example, many slaves who left Africa as Muslims; Islam had been established on the continent for centuries by the time the Americas were discovered and the Atlantic slave trade began. Once in the Americas, Muslims were given no leeway to practice their faith. Christianity was the only religious option, and it was all but mandatory.

In some other countries of the western hemisphere, notably Brazil and Cuba, enslaved peoples found ways to hold fast to some of their beliefs and traditions. The Yoruba people, from what is now Nigeria, had partial success. In Cuba and Brazil, they managed to fuse their religious tradition with Roman Catholicism in a way that was Catholic enough to satisfy the slave owners, but Yoruba enough to allow the slaves a sense of connection with their ancestors. These syncretic faiths came to be known as Santeria, candomblé, macumba—there are many names and many distinctions—and they basically involve associating specific Yoruba demigods, called orishas in Cuba and the other Spanish-speaking slave-owning islands, with specific Catholic saints. On the day that Catholics celebrated Saint Barbara, for example, the slaves joined in the acts of veneration—but unbeknownst to the slave owners, the Africans were actually honoring Shango, the Yoruba god of thunder, lightning, and virility.

Along with these beliefs, snippets of language survived. The standard greeting one gives to an Afro Cuban *babalawo*, or priest—*Iboru, iboya, ibocheche*—is said to be a corruption of a name given to a Yoruba deity that means "one who lives both in heaven and earth." Today officials of the various Afro Cuban and Afro Brazilian faiths hold ecumenical councils with Nigerian religious leaders. A certain continuity of identity was maintained.[6]

In the United States, nothing of the old religious belief system survived. This was perhaps because Protestantism lacked the Catholic emphasis on the pantheon of saints, which left the slaves no convenient way to practice their faiths surreptitiously. In the barrier islands along the South Carolina coast, a culture called Gullah still exists and is being studied and preserved; the creole that the Gullah people speak is a mash-up of archaic English and various West African tongues, and it is utterly incomprehensible to a nonspeaker. Beyond that one example, however, our ancestors' history was obliterated. In that sense, we really have no idea who we are.

Advances in genetic science do make it possible for African Americans to send away a DNA sample and get back a report offering some general idea of what region and ethnic group their ancestors came from. But after a lot of initial excitement about the prospect of being able to do *Roots* in a lab, it turns out that the testing might not be as precise as originally thought. To learn that one of your ancestors might have been a member of the Ibo ethnic group, for example, or that an ancestor might have come from the Angola region would be something. But it wouldn't be much—especially given that different laboratories often come up with different histories.

The African immigrants, by contrast, have family histories

that go back hundreds of years. They are proud of this heritage—and it shows. These are generalizations, but they are true: Native-born African Americans often envy the immigrants their deep historical knowledge and heritage, and immigrants often look down on the native-born for their rootlessness. These deep and seldom-expressed differences over identity, I believe, may underlie the shallower complaints that the two groups voice about each other. The native-born say that the immigrants are arrogant, and the immigrants say that the native-born have no pride in themselves.

In decades past, the process of incorporating immigrants fully into the African American community was natural, inevitable, and quick. Most of the newcomers were from the Caribbean, similarly disconnected from their ancient roots, and in any event they were black in a society that made no fine distinctions between people with dark skin. The formal and informal rules of Jim Crow segregation did not take into account country of national origin; there was no special section in the front of the bus for Jamaicans.

Today, immigrants from Africa can, if they choose, maintain a distinction. Ethiopians and Nigerians are both Africans, but they come from different ethnic groups, separated by the breadth of a continent, and they have radically different histories. They can insist on their individual national and cultural identities or they can feel a sense of common identity in being immigrants; they can stand apart from the native-born, or they can blend into the fabric of Mainstream black America.

The point is that they will have a choice. There can be different shades of black.

8

THE EMERGENT (PART 2): HOW BLACK IS BLACK?

The other segment of Emergent black America also faces issues of heritage and identity, but they are quite different: What if you knew that half of your history was written in Africa and the other half in England or Ireland or Germany or Sweden? What if you were biracial?

According to the way American society has always worked, you would still be black. But societies evolve, and this one is no exception. Do you now have the option of being white as well? Are you something in between? And who gets to decide, society or the individual?

There is a long backstory to this question of modern identity, and to understand it we can look at a society where the story began much like it did here but took a different turn: Brazil.

More than twelve million people were brought from Africa to the New World to work as slaves, roughly between 1500 and 1870, and more than 40 percent of them went to Brazil—far more than to the United States or any other country. The Portuguese colonists who crossed the ocean in search of fortune were overwhelmingly male, so there was a long history of miscegenation between settlers and female slaves. The same was true in this country, of course, but one important difference is that in Brazil—and in the rest of Latin America—the offspring of these black-white unions were considered not black or white but mulatto. This intermediate designation persisted after emancipation, and compared to the United States there was only a mild taboo against interracial marriage. Brazil today is characterized by racial disparities—white people, generally, are richer and more powerful than black people—but the question of who is "white" and who is "black" has been more a matter of skin color than family history.

In the United States, by contrast, the unwritten one-drop rule mandated that anyone with any African genetic heritage, visible or not, was "colored" or "Negro" or "black." As far as Jim Crow was concerned, no one was mulatto or biracial. If you had one black parent and one white parent, you were unambiguously and permanently black. If you happened to think otherwise—and decided, say, to use the "white" restroom or water fountain—you were soon instructed in the error of your ways.

That pattern has never changed, but now it might. Since interracial marriage was made legal throughout the country in 1967 and gradually became socially acceptable, what once was an anomaly has become commonplace. Stanford University sociologist Michael J. Rosenfeld estimated that the number of black-white interracial couples has increased fivefold since 1960, and that in 2000 about 7 percent of all married and cohabitating couples in the country were "interracial." While Asian-white and Hispanic-white marriages are more numerous, the frequency of black-white marriages—more "transgressive" of societal norms than other cross-couplings, according to Rosenfeld—is accelerating.[1]

A Pew Research Center survey, based on analysis of census data, found that in 2008, a full 22 percent of black male newlyweds married "outside their race." This reflects what Pew called a "stark" gender difference: Just 9 percent of black female newlyweds had embarked on interracial marriages.[2]

Race still matters in love and marriage, but it matters much less now than it did just a few decades ago. I attended the previously all-white Orangeburg High School in the late 1960s, and the students I got to know best were in the fast-track classes. There were not many girls who took the upper-level math and science courses. One who did was Kathy Kovacevich, who was from somewhere up north and didn't fully understand what race meant in my hometown. Once the two of us were working together on a project, and I gave her a ride to pick up some notes she had left at home. We walked into her house and I froze at the door—I remembered myself. I knew that for a young black man to be alone with a young white woman was asking for a world of trouble, even if I were just sitting on the couch and waiting while she found the papers she was looking for. What if her father came home while I was there? What if the neighbors had seen me go inside? At a minimum, she was risking social ostracism. At worst, I was risking life and limb.

Today this all sounds ridiculous. But back then, the idea of seeing an interracial couple walking down Russell Street, past the main square with its statue of a Confederate soldier, would have been as far-fetched as the notion of seeing a Martian and a Venusian strolling beneath the Spanish moss down by the Edisto River. The only difference is that the extraterrestrials wouldn't have risked a beating.

The reality was, of course, that interracial relationships took place all the time. In 2003, when it was revealed that Essie Mae Washington-Williams—a light-skinned black woman— was the daughter of arch-segregationist Strom Thurmond, and that she had attended South Carolina State University in Orangeburg, I called home to tell my family the news. "Oh, we thought you knew," my mother said. "Everybody knew. All the older people, I mean."

It turned out that a good friend and longtime coworker of my mother's had been at SCSU at the same time as Washington-Williams. She had told my mother—and everybody else in town, I guess—about the day when Thurmond had pulled up in a big sedan in front of a building on the SCSU campus and waited patiently until Washington-Williams came out and got into the car. They sped off, and the car brought her back to campus hours later. Apparently Thurmond visited his daughter fairly often and actually paid for her education. While he never could have publicly acknowledged her as family, privately he accepted his paternity and assumed at least some measure of parental responsibility. Since the relationship was not revealed until after Thurmond's death, no one had the chance to ask him about the obvious conflict between his die-hard insistence on separation of the races, which had been the basis of his failed presidential campaign, and his fatherly concern for the well-being of a child. Not for the first time, philosophy proved no match for biology.

Washington-Williams's mother was Carrie Butler, a servant in the household of Thurmond's parents. Butler was just sixteen when her daughter was born; Thurmond was twenty-two. This was the pattern of interracial relationships for much of American history—master-slave until the Civil War, then employer-servant afterward. In the South, these unions were almost exclusively between white men and black women. The determination of white Southerners to eliminate the possibility of sexual relations between the other variable in the matrix—black men and white women—was one of the foundational pillars of Jim Crow.

Naturally the unthinkable did happen—jazz musicians with their white groupies and patrons, Sammy Davis Jr. marrying May Britt. But such relationships were formed on the fringes of society, among entertainers, hipsters, hopheads, bon vivants, academics, and foreigners. In 1961, one such union, between an adventurous young student from the American heartland eager to discover the world and a brilliant but mercurial scholar from Kenya, produced the forty-fourth president of the United States.

The *Loving v. Virginia* decision in 1967, which legalized interracial marriage in the states where it was still illegal— Virginia, Alabama, Arkansas, Delaware, Florida, Georgia, Kentucky, Louisiana, Mississippi, Missouri, North Carolina, South Carolina, Oklahoma, Tennessee, Texas, West Virginia, and Maryland (which repealed its law after the suit was filed but before the court ruled)—was a huge step. Perhaps a more important event, that same year, was the Summer of Love in San Francisco, which marked the beginning of the American cultural revolution. For those young enough to tune in, turn on, and drop out, barriers such as race existed only to be overcome. The wild side existed only to be walked on. And for those who might not have felt compelled to make a political statement—or who, perhaps, had found other effective ways to annoy their parents—there was the simple circumstance of falling in love.

This once-forbidden love made possible the existence of Tiger Woods, Halle Berry, Derek Jeter, Mariah Carey, Alicia Keys—bold-faced names who are part of Emergent black America. It is difficult to tease out of census data an accurate figure for the number of black-white biracial Americans in the United States. My best guess, after looking at the data and making a few conservative assumptions, is at least two million. Whatever the number may be, I'm quite confident in predicting that it's about to soar.

The baby boomers were the first generation of African Americans to know desegregated schools and neighborhoods. Subsequent generations of Mainstream African Americans have known nothing else. To the boomers, race was important, inescapable, urgent. To their children, race means much less. There is no cultural gap between black children who grew up in suburban, middle-class settings and their white classmates from down the street. From kindergarten through high school, they are taught about tolerance and diversity; they don't just learn about Christmas, they decorate their classrooms for Hanukkah and Kwanzaa, too. Born mostly in the 1980s, this so-called millennial generation is as far removed from the tumult of the civil rights struggle as my generation is from the Great Depression. They can read about that time in history books, but there is no way that they could have a feeling for what it was like, no way that they could really connect.

The young people who are now in their twenties have had a radically different experience of race than my generation had. I wouldn't call it a "post-racial" generation, because to me that implies a denial that such a thing as race still exists. "Anti-racial" seems to me a better term, in that the millennials have heard one overriding lesson about the subject since they were in the cradle: Race doesn't matter. On college campuses, especially, the idea that race should in any way restrict any student's dating choices is viewed as antediluvian and weird. So far, this militant open-mindedness has not translated into an explosion of interracial marriage. It may be that while racial barriers to campus friendships, hookups, and other relationships have been all but eliminated, the search for a life partner is freighted with more societal baggage. Marriage inevitably brings families into the picture, and it may be the case that the millennials' parents, despite their pride in being members of the generation that changed the world, find that their political beliefs against racism of any kind are overmatched by history and culture—a stubborn inheritance that no one generation, not even the boomers, could possibly erase. But history's direction is clear, and the imperatives of human nature that compel young adults to fall in love and procreate are eternal. I'm confident that we are about to see an unprecedented wave of interracial marriages and the largest cohort of interracial children in American history.

In other words: I have seen the future, and it is beige.

* * *

I hesitate to return to a character who has already become quite familiar in these pages—President Barack Obama—but he is relevant in this chapter, too, because in addition to being the ultimate Transcendent black American, he is also a double Emergent. As the son of a Kenyan, he represents the internationalization of black America (although his father was part of a smaller, precursor trickle of black people from Africa and the Caribbean who were high-powered enough to gain entry before the immigration laws were changed). And, of course, he is also the son of a white woman from Kansas.

When he launched his campaign, Obama was seen—not by the African American public, generally, but by the national media—as perhaps insufficiently "black" to win black America's unconditional support. That quickly fizzled out—it was obvious that Obama's self-identification as a black American was complete and unambiguous, and in any event he didn't look like anyone who could ever be called "white" in the United States. Obama grew up mostly in Indonesia and Hawaii, so it was an act of conscious will for him to adopt his black American identity. That was how society was going to brand him whether he liked it or not, but he cultivated his black Americanness (American blackness?) with what looked almost like the zeal of a convert. His skin color and African facial features were always going to be there for everyone to see, and to categorize, but still he might have emerged from his adolescent search for himself as essentially colorless—deracinated, not just in the sense of being raceless but also rootless. He had to be black, but he didn't have to *act* black.

Instead, he evolved a persona that could best be described as black urban cool. He walks with an easy lope; he plays basketball, not tennis. On the occasions when I've seen him interact with groups that are mostly or exclusively black, he shows no hint of unfamiliarity with in-group gesture, mannerism, cadence, or tone. He strikes no false notes. It is difficult to spell out exactly what I mean, since it has so much to do with affect and vibe. Perhaps this helps: In any setting, if he chooses, he can effortlessly give the impression of someone walking into an upscale jazz club and gliding through the room toward his regular table.

The he's-too-black phase of Obama's campaign—courtesy of the Reverend Jeremiah Wright and his Trinity United Church of Christ—came a year after the not-black-enough phase. Both were ridiculous, but the too-black meme was a real threat to Obama's chance of winning the Democratic nomination. He responded by giving a remarkable speech in Philadelphia about race and how it fit into the broader American historical narrative. As rhetoric, as political theater, and as a display of erudition, it was stunning. But I was less interested in the broad sweep of Obama's speech than in a few lines that were intensely personal.

At that point, during the first Wright eruption, Obama was not yet ready to cut ties with his longtime pastor. He acknowledged Wright's failings, but he added:

> As imperfect as he may be, [Wright] has been like family to me. He strengthened my faith, officiated my wedding, and baptized my children . . .
>
> I can no more disown him than I can disown the black community. I can no more disown him than I can my white grandmother—a woman who helped raise me, a woman who sacrificed again and again for me, a woman who loves me as much as she loves anything in this world, but a woman who once confessed her fear of black men who passed by her on the street, and who on more than one occasion has uttered racial or ethnic stereotypes that made me cringe.[3]

Commentators who picked up on that line accused Obama of "throwing his grandmother under the bus" by alleging she made racist remarks. But I heard something much more interesting: the simple statement that while Obama was a black American, the fact that he was biracial meant that his relationship with white America was necessarily different from mine, in that it was personal. Obama might sit in a pew and listen to the Afrocentric "us versus them" fire and brimstone of Wright's preaching, but he could never fully buy into it. At a fundamental level, for Obama the conflict would have had to be "us versus us," or even "me versus me." For anyone who wants to avoid crippling self-loathing and years of psychoanalysis, it's best not to go there.

This is the real question posed by Emergent black America: Do the rapidly increasing numbers of immigrant and biracial African Americans have the same sense of historical injury that other black Americans do? And if not, does it matter? Might it change the atmosphere, and perhaps lower the temperature as well?

I'm reminded of Obama's observation, in my Oval Office interview, that soon—if it is not already the case—there will be more African Americans who have no experience of Jim Crow racism than those who do. This is an important milestone because memories of those pre-enlightened times are more stubborn, more vivid, and more ambiguous in their psychological impact than many people might think. A rough equivalent, I suppose, would be having survived and escaped an abusive relationship. Nobody would choose to go through that kind of trauma, and nobody would wish such an experience for their son or daughter. But having endured and overcome the abuse, one learns. One becomes cautious. One does not give trust or commit lightly. And one never, ever forgets.

When I was growing up, sometimes it seemed as if white

folks spent most of their waking hours trying to think up new ways to keep black people down. Given the time and place, South Carolina in the early '60s, that wasn't far from the truth. When the Voting Rights Act gave black people access to the polls, for example, white officials simply gerrymandered the city limits—including white suburban developments, excluding black ones—to ensure that African Americans could not take power at city hall. Any reasonable person would conclude that the great legislative triumphs of 1964 and 1965, as monumental as they were, didn't represent the end of the struggle. They marked the beginning of a new phase in which the adversary would fight with subtlety and nuance, not with burning crosses.

It was easy for some African Americans to slip into something resembling paranoia—indeed, my colleague at *The Washington Post*, columnist Richard Cohen, once cautioned me to remember that "the word 'paranoid' has no meaning for blacks and Jews." After Dr. King was killed, did "they" purposely allow the black commercial centers of major cities to burn, thus setting back the quest for economic empowerment? Was it an accident that the heroin and crack epidemics raged in the inner cities but not in the white suburbs?

I never put stock in conspiracy theories, simply because my experience as a reporter taught me that it's almost impossible for three or four people to pull off any kind of secret plot; that there could be thousands or even millions of coconspirators, and that they could keep quiet for decades, is beyond fantasy. But I know that the experience of Jim Crow has left me with a hard little nugget of suspicion and resentment buried deep inside, and that it gives me motivation and strength. It's the feeling that there are people out there who don't want me to succeed, which makes me all the more determined to deny them satisfaction.

African Americans of my generation transmit some of this legacy to our children, either consciously or unconsciously. It's like passing down through the family a suit of armor—an heirloom that protects but also burdens. But the fastest-growing segments of black America—the Emergents—have less reason, or perhaps no reason at all, to go through life wearing chain mail.

For black immigrants from Africa and the Caribbean, the United States may be judged guilty of modern sins, but not the ancient kind that fester in the blood. Immigrants may have complicated feelings about the European colonial powers, but America is seen as an imperfect society that nevertheless offers economic opportunity and political freedom—seen in this light unambiguously, with no historical asterisk. Why else would Jamaicans and Bahamians be so eager to come to this country to join the family members who came before them? Why would Ethiopians or Nigerians leave their homelands and move halfway around the world?

The immigrants are anything but ignorant about America's racial history, but they arrive at the theater in the middle of the third act. They don't enter a country that trains fire hoses on black people, they enter one that practices affirmative action and makes a special effort to enroll their children in the best colleges. They don't enter a country that is obviously hostile to black entrepreneurs, they enter one with minority set-asides and small-business loans. The American dream doesn't look like a cinch, but neither does it look like a cruel deception.

I don't want to overstate. The men, women, and children

who constitute Emergent black America have no immunity from racial discrimination. If they want to feel a sense of community, they are more likely to seek it—and find it—among the four black Americas than elsewhere. And anyone who might believe that immigrant status confers any degree of protection from the most corrosive residues of history should remember what happened to Abner Louima and Amadou Diallo, two black men, at the hands of New York City police. In 1997, Louima, who was born in Haiti, was arrested outside a Brooklyn nightclub, taken to a station house, and brutalized by officers, including being sodomized with a broken broomstick. Two years later, Diallo, an immigrant from Guinea, was killed—shot nineteen times—as he stood at the front door of his Bronx apartment house; police said they thought he was reaching for a gun, but Diallo, unarmed, was actually trying to take out his wallet and identify himself to the officers. Every black man in America knows he is more likely to be the victim of police brutality or mistaken identity than his white coworker in the next cubicle—every black man, no matter where he was born.

But there is a difference for Emergents. No matter how completely and unambiguously I feel a part of the American system, I know that this system despised my parents, and their parents, and the rest of my ancestors stretching back nearly four hundred years. This knowledge isn't oppressive or even particularly intrusive; I don't really think about it, and it certainly doesn't affect the way I go about my day. But it's there, and I don't think I could help feeling differently if I were from an immigrant family whose history was written thousands of miles away.

And biracial Americans? Obama's insight was valuable:

How is it possible to hold a class of people in contempt—even historical contempt—if your grandmother and grandfather are among them? A generalization such as "white people want to keep black people down" has no meaning if a white mother or father, white aunts and uncles, white grandparents and perhaps white great-grandparents bounced you on their knees.

If current trends hold, most biracial black-and-white Americans will continue to self-identify as African American. But a sense of being somehow divorced, or at least estranged, from the larger society cannot possibly come easily to them. This is a good thing—less racial tension is a goal that we all should be able to agree on. And as the numbers of the Emergent grow, the posture of black America toward the rest of America will evolve—while the once-bright line between black America and the rest of America becomes fuzzy and hard to pin down.

"Funny, he doesn't look Jewish" may be joined by a new observation: "Funny, he doesn't seem black."

9 URGENCY, FOCUS, AND SACRIFICE

Every year, the National Urban League issues *The State of Black America Report*. Big enough to serve as a doorstop, the document (referred to as SOBA) is a voluminous, meticulously researched assessment of where African Americans stand compared to the larger society. There are narrative sections that seek to establish context. "The response to the devastation caused by near-record high unemployment for African Americans that threatens to push an already struggling community deeper into poverty and despair must be urgent," said the Executive Summary of SOBA 2010. "Jobs with living wages and good benefits must be the primary goal for 2010 and ahead." But the main focus was, as always, a number: 71.8.[1]

Urban League researchers compile and analyze data from a variety of sources to calculate the Equality Index—a number meant to quantify precisely where black America stands in comparison to white America. Averaging scores in subcategories that include economics, health, education, social justice, and civic engagement, the Urban League reported that African Americans had attained 71.8 percent of parity with white

Americans. This was the first time in four years that the number had shown improvement; for 2009, it had been 71.2.

SOBA is an impressive piece of work, assembled with great care. But what does it really mean? In 2010 did it mean that I, and every other black citizen, should have felt that the turning of the year brought us precisely .6 percent closer to attaining the American dream?

Imagine a household in which half the men are professional basketball players and half are professional jockeys. A State of the Family report would calculate that the men, on average, are five feet eleven inches tall. But that would hardly tell the whole story. In fact, it would tell the wrong story.

There are approximately forty million African Americans[2]—more people than live, for example, in Canada, Argentina, Algeria, or Poland. If we were discussing any of those countries, we wouldn't hesitate to evaluate the circumstances of different economic, social, and cultural sectors. We would consider the rich and the poor, the working class and the middle class, the native-born and the immigrant. Not doing so would be superficial, like confining ourselves to observing that one country was colored blue on the map and another was colored pink.

Averages and medians can lie. Crude statistics give the impression that the past four decades have seen uneven social progress and only modest economic gains by African Americans. A huge increase in college attendance and graduation rates is partly offset by incongruously high dropout and incarceration rates. The African American poverty rate has fallen, but black family incomes barely seem to have budged at all in comparison to those of whites. The median black household earns about 62 percent of what the median white household earns, roughly the same ratio that was measured four decades ago. That's what the numbers seem to say—yet it could hardly be more obvious that African Americans have seen tremendous advancement and unprecedented change. The affluent neighborhoods of Prince George's County are not a figment of the collective imagination. The election of Barack Obama was not just a dream.

Forty years of disintegration have, in fact, produced a miracle. A thriving black middle class has been created, a group that has not yet reached full parity with white America but has come remarkably close. If you look only at two-parent households, for example, African American families now earn about 85 percent of what white families earn.[3] It is wrong to minimize this lingering disparity and right to insist that we find ways to eliminate it, but it's nonsensical to ignore the tremendous gains that Mainstream black America has made.

The purchasing power of African Americans was on track to surpass $1 trillion in 2012 before the recession took hold; that milestone may be delayed, but surely not for long. A study conducted for the Magazine Publishers of America found that African Americans are particularly avid consumers. Looking at the habits of young people—who are most coveted by advertisers—the study found that black teens spend more on average than white teens for a number of products, including clothes, video-game hardware, computer software, and casual shoes. Black teens are especially loyal to their favorite brands, and they have greater-than-average influence over household purchases of items from cereal to cell phones.[4]

Because of desegregation and disintegration, the black middle class is not only bigger and wealthier but also liberated from the separate but unequal nation called black America that existed before the triumph of civil rights. The black

Mainstream is now woven into the fabric of America, not just economically but culturally as well. The Mainstream has a distinct identity—a clear sense of itself as African American—and clings determinedly to its historic institutions, like the historically black churches, universities, fraternities, and sororities that were so vital during the long, dark night of Jim Crow. The Mainstream also has a tendency to cluster together in black-majority enclaves, no longer out of necessity but out of choice. But to the extent that any of this might be portrayed as an unusual clannishness or tendency toward self-segregation, such an assessment would be objectively wrong: It turns out that whites are considerably more likely to live in racially segregated neighborhoods than blacks.

Socially, economically, and culturally, the black Mainstream is part of the American mainstream. Middle-class African Americans buy too much on credit and save too little for the future, they burden their children with high and often unrealistic expectations, they drive automobiles that are excessively large and wasteful, they become emotionally attached to professional sports teams made up of wealthy, spoiled, indifferent athletes—in short, they behave just like other Americans. Even though there is still ground to be made up, it is fair to say that for all intents and purposes, Mainstream African Americans have arrived.

The Abandoned, however, have not. And the question is whether they ever will.

* * *

As the Mainstream have risen, the Abandoned have fallen. To be black, poor, and uneducated in America is, arguably, a more desperate and intractable predicament today than it was forty or fifty years ago.

I say "arguably" because in terms of material possessions and physical living conditions there has been obvious improvement. Housing is less squalid and overcrowded than it once was for poor black people. The wholesale transfer of manufacturing to China robbed unskilled American workers of jobs, but that phenomenon, plus the rise of discount retailers like Wal-Mart, drove prices so low that former luxuries came within reach of practically everyone—televisions, household appliances, mobile phones, flashy "gold" jewelry made out of nickel or zinc. The poor certainly don't *look* as poor as they once did.

But in most other ways, the situation and prospects of the Abandoned black poor have worsened. There is no need to list, once again, all the many interlocking problems and crises that afflict impoverished African American urban and rural communities. It suffices to ask one question: How is a teenager living in Abandoned dysfunction today supposed to escape? By following the sage advice of parents and other mentors? The teenager is likely being raised by a single mother, who herself was raised by a single mother. By attending first-class public schools, with constructive academic support at home? We know all about the failings of big-city public education. By landing a blue-collar industrial job with security, benefits, and a middle-class wage? Those jobs can be found in China or Brazil, not in Cincinnati or Boston. The ladder that generations have used to climb out of poverty is missing its rungs.

Somehow opportunity has to be created where it does not now exist. But first, there is another factor to take into account:

personal responsibility. Opening doors only helps those who are ready to walk through.

Not even the most foggy-headed or starry-eyed could deny that wrong choices play a huge role in keeping the Abandoned mired in their plight—and that no policies or programs can possibly succeed unless individuals make better choices. This was the basic message of *Come On, People*, the book by Bill Cosby and Alvin Poussaint that stridently lectured poor African Americans on the need to change their ways. The authors didn't deserve all the criticism they got—for the most part they were just stating, or screaming, the obvious. They pointed out that there is an alarming crisis among black men in this country, and urged young men to do better—to stay in school, cut out the violence, stop fathering children out of wedlock, and generally behave like "real men" instead of caricatures. They advised black women to "hang in there" and provide support that might help change black men's erring ways. They spoke of the need for community and denounced the prohibition, applied with deadly force in some Abandoned neighborhoods, against cooperating with police to help get offenders off the streets. They reminded readers of African Americans' rich history of struggle and triumph, presenting this legacy as an inspiration. They wrote about parenthood and effective child-raising—the responsibilities, the frustrations, the joys. They wrote about the vital importance of education as a means of uplift and escape. Cosby and Poussaint were accused of blaming the victim, but nothing they said was gratuitous or untrue.

In the end, though, *Come On, People* didn't have the galvanizing effect that its authors must have hoped for. It wasn't that they were trying to sell the wrong message but that they failed to get through to their intended audience. The book became fodder for passionate talk-show debates. But to the extent that it reached African Americans, the book connected with Mainstream readers. They could either agree with the prescriptions that Cosby and Poussaint outlined, or they could complain that these Transcendent authors were letting the larger society, including inattentive elected officials, off the hook. Meanwhile, in the dysfunctional Abandoned communities that the authors were trying to reach, *Come On, People* probably made less of an impression than a particularly entertaining episode of *Judge Judy*.

Increasingly, between the Abandoned and the rest of black America, there is a failure to communicate, much less comprehend.

One place where everyone comes together is black radio, where hosts such as Tom Joyner, Michael Baisden, Steve Harvey, Mo'Nique, and Yolanda Adams aggregate audiences that are economically and socially diverse. In 2006, when a group of African American teenagers in Louisiana—the so-called "Jena Six"—were made to face what seemed to be unfairly tough criminal charges after a school fight against white students, Baisden and other African American hosts were instrumental in organizing large protests that drew national attention to the case. But the case looked like a simple, old-fashioned instance of racial discrimination and unequal justice—the kind of thing all four black Americas see in more or less the same light. Day in and day out, black radio hosts do an admirable job of examining the plight of the Abandoned from every conceivable angle. The truth is, though, that they have little impact on either policy or behavior. The gap is just too wide for their reach.

On Easter Sunday 2010, President Obama and his family went to church at Allen Chapel AME Church in Washington, a lively congregation in one of the Abandoned neighborhoods east of the Anacostia River. The pastor, Reverend Michael Bell, called the presidential visit "a monumental moment for us as a community." Worshippers had begun lining up before dawn to make it through all the levels of security screening. The Obamas sang, clapped, and rejoiced on the holiest day of the Christian calendar, and then their twenty-two-car motorcade sped back across the Anacostia to the picture-postcard part of town, where the cherry blossoms were gloriously in bloom.

Just a few days earlier, driving past a street corner not many blocks from Allen Chapel, gunmen in a minivan had sprayed bullets into a crowd of people gathered outside a decrepit little apartment building. When all was over, four young black men and women had been killed and five others injured in what was described as the worst mass shooting in Washington in years. The city was stunned, both by the scale and the senselessness of the carnage. Then came outrage and anger at the needless loss of human life and potential; one of those fatally shot was a sixteen-year-old girl, an aspiring chef who by all accounts was full of talent and ambition, but who picked the wrong evening to meet some of her friends at a popular gathering spot. As the story behind the shooting began to emerge, the city's anger seemed to give way to hopelessness and resignation. The pathology involved was so deep and multilayered that it was hard to know where to begin.

According to police, the story began a week before the mass shooting, when a young man's "gold-tone" bracelet went missing. The bracelet owner believed he knew who had taken it, so he and his brother went to find the alleged thief, a twenty-year-old man. When they found him, they allegedly shot him dead. The bracelet owner was subsequently arrested and charged with the alleged thief's murder.

The bracelet owner's brother was not apprehended. A few days later, someone shot him in the face—probably as an act of revenge or street justice, police theorize. The shooting actually was more of a grazing, and the brother was not seriously injured.

The alleged thief's funeral was an all-day affair, involving a church service downtown, burial at a local cemetery, and finally a repast for family and friends. Some of those friends gathered later at the corner of South Capitol and Brandywine, in front of that decrepit little apartment building—a convenient spot, across from a modest commercial strip, which was known as a safe, no-beefs-allowed demilitarized zone between the territories of several drug-selling "crews."

The bracelet owner's brother and several of his friends, meanwhile, were allegedly cruising the streets on their own mission of justice or revenge. Police say they rented a minivan and went first to a housing project and shot one man, apparently believing that he had some connection to the bracelet affair. Then the shooters happened to drive down South Capitol Street, a major thoroughfare, and recognized some of the alleged thief's friends among the post-funeral crowd.

Through the open windows of the minivan came a deadly spray of indiscriminate gunfire from at least two pistols and an AK-47-style assault weapon. It is not clear whether the intended targets of the rampage were among the nine people who fell. It is possible that the bracelet owner's brother, still nursing his face wound, was aiming for his assailant. It is possible that the shooters wanted to eliminate someone who might testify against the bracelet owner at his eventual trial. It is also possible that the shooters believed someone in the crowd had cooperated with police in identifying and apprehending the bracelet owner for allegedly killing the alleged thief. In tit-for-tat violent disputes like this one, "snitching" is a capital offense.

The assailants led police on a wild, action-movie-style chase that sped into nearby Prince George's County, where three police cars crashed in a spectacular accident, and then back into Washington. Finally the assailants were cornered and caught. The brother of the bracelet owner and another man were charged with murder. Later a third man was arrested on murder charges and a fourth on gun charges for allegedly supplying the assault rifle. All the suspects were black men between the ages of twenty and twenty-six.[5]

After Obama's visit to the neighborhood, I went out to the site of the shooting. There I saw an all-too-familiar tableau—a mound of flowers and teddy bears, an impromptu memorial to the dead. In front of a habitually ignored NO LOITERING sign, there was a collection of liquor bottles—probably a special tribute to one or more of the dead from fellow members of a "crew," which is the euphemism that authorities in Washington use when they talk about gangs. I went back to my office to write a column, but I could not find anything original to say. There was the contrast between the presidential visit and the shooting, between hope and hopelessness. But beyond that, what else? What should have happened so that there would have been no sad, improvised memorial on that corner for me to visit? If we could have turned back the clock to keep nine people from being shot, and four of them from dying, what moment would we have chosen in which to intervene? Just before the minivan drove up? Before the bracelet was stolen? Even then would have been too late. The time to avert the killings was before any of the young men involved—as assailants, victims, or both—came to understand that a missing ten-dollar bracelet was reason to kill or be killed.

Obama did not speak at the Easter service, and some critics complained that he should have taken to the pulpit and preached about the killings. I'm not sure what he could have said, though, beyond acknowledging the tragedy and expressing the same shock, horror, outrage, and regret that everyone already felt. Between the White House and Anacostia, the president had traveled just a few miles. But the distance might as well have been measured in light-years.

Sociologist Elijah Anderson, whose 1999 book, *Code of the Street*, helped explain why some low-income young people make choices that seem illogical or self-defeating, has written that "the story of the inner-city black community . . . is at heart one of profound isolation—economic, physical, and social."[6] Just as a remote island will develop an ecosystem that is functional but perhaps radically different from that of the mainland, so did Abandoned black America—increasingly isolated from the Mainstream—develop a cultural ecosystem that makes sense internally but nowhere else. Outsiders do not often get to see the private behavior that is not just familiar but universal: a mother's tenderness as she combs her young daughter's hair, a boy's nervous indecision as he chooses an outfit for his first day of high school. What we see instead is public behavior that often seems bizarrely self-defeating.

Anderson studied inner-city Philadelphia (which happens to be Bill Cosby's hometown). In a 1998 essay, "The Social Ecology of Youth Violence," he explained:

Almost everyone in poor inner-city neighborhoods is struggling financially and therefore feels a certain distance from the rest of America, but there are degrees of alienation, captured by the labels "decent" and "street." Residents use these labels as judgments on themselves or others. People of both orientations often coexist in the same extended family. There is also a great deal of "code-switching": a person may exhibit both decent and street orientations, depending on the occasion. Decent people, especially young people, put a premium on the ability to code-switch. They share many of the "decent" middle-class values of the wider society, but know that the open display of such values carries little weight on the street: it does not provide the emblems that say "I can take care of myself." So they develop a repertoire of behaviors that provide that security. Those who are "street," having had less exposure to the wider society, may have difficulty code-switching. They are strongly imbued with the code of the street and either do not know the rules for decent behavior or may see little value in displaying such knowledge.[7]

In Anderson's lexicon, both "decent" and "street" families in Abandoned black communities understand that they are essentially on their own—and that because of their isolation and estrangement from the larger society, following the "code" is a more urgent imperative than living up to middle-class expectations. "At the heart of the code is the issue of respect—loosely defined as being treated 'right' or being granted . . . the deference one deserves," Anderson wrote.[8] Failure to demand the proper respect is seen as weakness—an invitation to further mistreatment.

This means that not even minor slights can be ignored. Stepping on someone's foot or bumping someone's shoulder while passing on the sidewalk can lead to words or even a fight. Maintaining eye contact for too long is seen as an act of aggression. In public, it is never seen as wise to confront the world with anything other than one's game face. In that sense, life is like one long ride on the New York City subway.

This heightened appreciation of respect and disrespect sometimes works in counterintuitive ways. Anderson described an episode he witnessed in inner-city Philadelphia. On a busy street, a woman stopped her car—entirely blocking a lane of traffic—and waited ten minutes for a man, perhaps a husband or boyfriend, to come out of a barbershop. In the suburbs, impatient drivers would have honked their horns and flashed their lights until the offending car moved out of the way. But in North Philadelphia, no one complained; drivers simply maneuvered around the woman's car and went about their business. The calculation was that to challenge her would provoke a confrontation because the woman—or her male friend—would feel compelled to respond with defiance. The inconvenience the woman had caused wasn't worth a potential conflict in which no one would be able to back down.[9]

For young people especially, material possessions, such as the most fashionable brand-name clothing and jewelry, are important because they command respect. The same is true in Mainstream society, of course, but the stakes are higher in communities where people struggle to afford necessities, let alone luxuries. Any teenager who obtains and flaunts high-status items—the *right* North Face jacket, for example, or the *right* Timberland boots—has to be willing and able to defend them. Taking such accoutrements by intimidation or force from the owner is the kind of bold action that can enhance another young man's status among his peers, and in turn provide inoculation against those who might be tempted to try something like that with him.

"Every young person in deprived inner-city black neighborhoods must learn to live with the code of the street," Anderson wrote. "The street kids must prove their manhood and achieve their identity under the intricate rules of the code. The decent kids must learn to coexist with it."[10]

The value system in Abandoned communities has a certain internal logic, but it plays an enormous role in separating the Abandoned from the Mainstream and everyone else. Mainstream youths may listen to the same music, wear the same clothes, and even make a show of displaying the same don't-mess-with-me attitude, but there's a difference between simply listening to violent or misogynistic hip-hop lyrics and actually accepting them as authentic, nonfiction narrative.

To dwell on violence, or the threat of violence, is of course unfair to the great majority of African Americans in Abandoned communities who are law-abiding, churchgoing citizens seeking only a better life for themselves and their families. Never, in more than three decades as a journalist, have I gone into a dangerous housing project or driven down a godforsaken country road and met a mother who did not love her children and want the best for them. I have met mothers and fathers who were ignorant of how to instruct their children and provide for them, but none who did not want to do so.

Since Lyndon Johnson's War on Poverty was allowed to peter out in the 1980s, government policies have essentially left the Abandoned to their own devices. The absence of work and the disintegration of the public schools eliminated traditional routes of advancement; knowing that there were no good jobs and that the schools were dysfunctional made people apathetic and resigned. Still, the unwritten code of insult, umbrage, and retribution that holds sway in Abandoned communities—enforced by a few, but followed by many—plays an enormously destructive role by choking off ambition and creating an atmosphere of randomness and uncertainty.

Those capable of code-switching have a chance of leaping the chasm—those who understand, for example, that while "acting white" in school is seen as a sign of softness and weakness, it is possible to avoid showing vulnerability in public and at the same time earn the kind of grades that make it possible to go to college. Those who cannot live in both worlds, who do not understand both sets of values, are all but lost.

The essential, and tragic, problem is that "keeping it real"—adhering to the code—requires either engaging in all manner of self-defeating behavior or finding elaborate subterfuges to avoid shooting oneself in the foot. The warping of values in Abandoned black America means that being successful requires being duplicitous—being literally two-faced. And that is never an easy way to live.

* * *

Some call it trickle-down, some talk about a rising tide lifting all boats. Whatever metaphor you use for Ronald Reagan's notion of how to run an economy, it obviously hasn't worked for low-income African Americans. I would argue that it hasn't worked for poor, working-class, or middle-class

Americans of any race, creed, or color, for that matter. In the past three decades, the economy has seen enormous growth and wealth-creation—but in boom-and-bust cycles that have destroyed too many industries, communities, and families. Middle-class incomes have been as stagnant as an algae-choked pond, while a Niagara of income has cascaded onto the wealthy and the superrich. It is ironic when the wealthy complain of having to shoulder an increasing share of the nation's overall tax burden. Surely they realize that this is because they have an increasing share of the money.

Worsening income distribution has been accompanied by a decline in economic and social mobility, once our nation's great pride and still a cherished element of the American dream. To be born poor and rise to wealth is now a much more difficult and less common feat in the United States than it was forty or fifty years ago, when industries such as automobile and steel factories provided a path into the middle class and working-class families could easily afford public higher education for their children. It is also increasingly difficult for someone born rich to fall into poverty—although this kind of downward mobility is more common for African Americans than for whites or any other group.

The recession brought on by the bursting of the housing bubble in 2007 demonstrated how precarious the situation of the middle class has become—and how much more tenuous middle-class status is for the black Mainstream. While joblessness overall climbed just past 10 percent, unemployment for African Americans surpassed 16 percent; among young black men in Abandoned neighborhoods, the rate was as high as 50 percent.[11] Black homeowners were disproportionately likely to find themselves trapped in mortgages they could not pay or legally committed to paying far more than their houses were currently worth, and thus became disproportionately likely to suffer foreclosures and evictions.

Meanwhile there is a widespread sense that the things that knit this country together—our political system, our infrastructure, our sense of community—have fallen into disrepair. The ethic of enlightened self-interest works brilliantly for running a capitalist economic system, but a nation is more than its economy. Nationhood also means shared ideals and values, a shared history, and shared resources.

Among African Americans, the successful have always evinced a determination to reach back and bring along the less fortunate. In my lifetime, I have met very few black professionals who did not feel it was their duty to mentor young African Americans and help advance their careers. I have met few African American professionals who do not try in some way to encourage and uplift the Abandoned, perhaps through mentoring programs at their churches, perhaps through volunteer organizations such as Concerned Black Men or the National Council of Negro Women, perhaps through fraternities or sororities. There is a long tradition in black communities of taking in, and caring for, children whose parents are unable to do so. Before disintegration, these organic, informal efforts might have been enough. But no more—not, at least, for the Abandoned.

A black senior vice president at a Fortune 500 firm might be able to significantly increase diversity by hiring and promoting qualified African Americans. But those qualified job applicants are going to come from the ranks of the Mainstream, not the Abandoned. Volunteer and nonprofit organizations have a tremendously beneficial impact on the lives of underprivileged young men and women, but are unable to give them all of what they desperately need—good schools, safe streets, positive parental supervision—and unable to erase the damage that has already been done.

The Transcendent and the Mainstream will continue to do whatever they can. But it is time to be realistic. We are winning lots of individual battles, but we are losing the war. And this fact—that we are losing ground with the Abandoned, rather than gaining ground—raises an issue that many Americans understandably wish would just go away: the future of affirmative action.

It is tempting to celebrate the success of the Mainstream, the advent of the Emergent, and the rise of the Transcendent by declaring affirmative action a thing of the past. The goal, after all, is to reach Dr. King's long-dreamed-of promised land where the legitimate criterion for judging a person is character, not color. It goes against the grain of America's values—or at least offends America's self-image—to deliberately and overtly prefer one group over another. The nation learned the rhetoric of the civil rights movement well, and those same stirring words are now recited on behalf of those who believe that affirmative action does harm to whites: Everyone is equal, discrimination is against the law, fairness is fundamental, unfairness is un-American.

The Obama presidency adds an exclamation point to these complaints. An African American is now the most powerful man in the country—in fact, the most powerful man in the world. For some who have long criticized affirmative action on philosophical grounds, the symbolism of seeing the Obama family in the White House provides the perfect visual to underscore their argument. For others, whose objection to preferential measures is more visceral, Obama's election suggests a more direct question: What more could you people possibly want?

These critics and complainers are actually right, in the long run. But they are premature.

I am a firm believer in the necessity for continued race-based affirmative action. It needs to be modified and modernized, but it should not be eliminated, not yet. I see three reasons. First, there is the historical injury that African Americans have suffered. Many people would like to put all of that behind us—to say, in effect, "All right, we tore down the legal barriers four decades ago and we gave black Americans a leg up. Now we're even-steven. Starting here and now, everybody has to compete for everything on an equal basis, with no preference asked for and none given. That's the American way." This view is understandable and in many ways attractive, but it is also superficial and wrong. Why would anyone expect forty years of redress, at times grudging and halfhearted, to offset nearly four hundred years of deliberate, comprehensive oppression? That so many African Americans have left poverty and ignorance behind, in spite of all the roadblocks and hurdles, is a miracle. But the miracle is still incomplete.

Second, racism and discrimination are radically diminished but not eliminated. In some studies, researchers have found that white employers often prefer white job applicants over black applicants who have clearly superior credentials. In at least one study, employers even chose a white job-seeker with a criminal record over a black man with no record and better qualifications. Aside from whatever overt prejudice remains, psychologists have done startling research on unconscious bias—for example, a documented tendency of test subjects to associate white faces with positive concepts and black faces with negative ones. This reflex may be conditioned by societal cues, but there are some researchers who believe, controversially, that a preference for light over dark might somehow be hardwired into the human brain. I find this far-fetched—at least I hope it's far-fetched—and I think it's more likely that humans may somehow be programmed to have an affinity with people who look like "us" rather than "them." This effect has been measured to be relatively small, and given how the definition of "us" has widened during my lifetime—"we who are affluent," "we who are middle class," "we who live in the suburbs," "we who play golf," "we who work in the same office," "we who see one another at social events," and many other "we's" now include black people—I have to assume that someday unconscious bias will just fade away. But for the present, it can only make the overt racism that remains more difficult to eradicate.

Third, affirmative action is an investment in America's future. As the nation becomes increasingly diverse, it is in no one's interest to have historically underprivileged groups feeling left out and resentful. And in a global economy that becomes more competitive by the day, where intellectual firepower is as important as military might, a mind really is a terrible thing to waste.

None of this is meant to deny, however, that indeed there has been a miracle. Proof lies in the existence of the Mainstream and the emergence of the Transcendent. It simply is not possible to defend the position that in a college admissions process incorporating affirmative action, the child of, say, Will Smith and Jada Pinkett Smith should be treated exactly the same as the child of a custodian and a nurse's aide. Affirmative action does two things: It compensates for inequality and bias, past and present; and it creates diversity. Transcendent black America should be ruled out for affirmative action except the kind that rich and powerful white Americans have been enjoying all along—"legacy" admission to elite schools, a la George W. Bush, because Daddy went there; plum sinecures in corporate America, like Dick Cheney's at Halliburton, that only come from spending quality time in the boardroom or on the golf course with the right people; and, of course, the Park Avenue equivalent of Head Start: a lightly taxed inheritance.

Whether Mainstream black America should continue to benefit from affirmative action is a subtler and more difficult question. On the merits alone, I would argue that it should. The Mainstream's gains are historic, but they are precarious; it will take at least another generation, and perhaps more, to significantly close the wealth gap that leaves Mainstream black Americans, in tough economic times, far too likely to fall and crash. But this is not a question that will be resolved solely on merit. Politics, resources, and priorities demand to be taken into account.

Politically, it is increasingly untenable to tell a middle-class white family that a middle-class black family across town, with an identical income, is going to be given advantages because of race. Demographic changes—the fact that in some of our biggest states, including California and Texas, whites are no longer a majority—makes affirmative action programs that are based solely on race vulnerable to attacks that they do nothing more than favor one minority over another. Realistically, a political consensus for blunt-instrument affirmative action no longer exists. President Obama dabbled with this idea during the campaign, saying that his daughters, Sasha and Malia, wouldn't deserve any special help when it was time for them to apply to college. But he didn't quite finish the thought. Sooner or later, I believe, he will have to. The fact is that whether the issue is jobs, college admissions, government contracts, or whatever, there will only be so much largesse to go around. Given that context, the big question is one of priorities.

I am convinced that affirmative action must be narrowed and intensified to be used as a tool to uplift the Abandoned. That means eliminating its benefits for African Americans above some specified income level.

This would be a real change. The biggest beneficiaries of affirmative action over the past four decades have been women—mostly white women—who occupy a place in the workforce and the academy that previous generations could not have imagined. (When the feminist revolution came, black women already worked for a living.) Second, in terms of gains, have been middle-class African Americans.

When affirmative action programs were launched—goals to diversify college admissions, minority hiring and training programs in many industries, set-aside programs to make sure that minority-owned firms won government contracts, and other such initiatives—opportunities naturally went to those who were best prepared to seize them. In pre-disintegration black America, families with relatively more money and relatively more education—the proto-Mainstream—rushed through the newly opened doors of admissions quotas and minority training programs. The poorest and least educated— the proto-Abandoned—were largely beyond the reach of affirmative action. As disintegration progressed, Abandoned neighborhoods fell apart, public school systems were allowed to collapse, and families with resources decided to move away.

All this just reinforced the pattern in which affirmative action favored the Mainstream. Black suburban enclaves, like Country Club Hills south of Chicago or the affluent neighborhoods northeast of St. Louis, were born—and affirmative action, to this day, helps sustain them. While most programs based on numerical quotas are no longer allowed, governments still have initiatives in place to ensure that minority firms participate in contracts; universities work around Supreme Court decisions to continue ensuring diversity in admissions; and most large corporations have made explicit commitments to increase diversity in hiring and promotions.

Meanwhile, Abandoned black America slid beyond a state of crisis to a condition of literal hopelessness. What is needed now is true affirmative action—policies and programs that reach those who need it most. These new initiatives will have to go far beyond the efforts that universities and employers now make to promote diversity; smart CEOs and university presidents, with an eye toward the demographic future, will continue these efforts anyway. What is needed is a kind of Marshall Plan for the Abandoned—massive intervention in education, public safety, health, and other aspects of life, with the aim being to arrest the downward spiral. Otherwise, that phrase I detest—permanent underclass—will become our permanent reality.

Taking the Mainstream out of the affirmative action equation would inevitably call attention to the competition that is already taking place between the Abandoned and the immigrant Emergent, who—like my friend Sentayu, the gym attendant with the brilliant daughter—would qualify for means-tested assistance. There is already friction between the two groups. Some advocates for the Abandoned say that immigrants should not qualify for affirmative action at all, since they have suffered no historical oppression—on American soil, at least—that merits redress. Meanwhile, immigrants have groused to me that the native-born Abandoned have all the power they need to take charge of their own lives and futures, but that they choose not to do so. The immigrants argue that if their children live in the same troubled neighborhoods, attend the same failed schools, overcome language and cultural barriers, and still end up as their class valedictorians and win scholarships to attend exclusive universities, their achievements should not be marginalized or in any sense diminished with an asterisk—that black immigrant success should be celebrated as an example of how to climb out of dysfunctional surroundings and vault into the Mainstream and beyond.

My view is that affirmative action programs are, by their nature, fairly blunt instruments, and that to try to add national origin as a criterion would be unwieldy at best and probably unworkable. I also believe it would be more trouble than it is worth. If the success of families from Nigeria, Ethiopia, Barbados, and elsewhere at climbing out of poverty suggests that the Abandoned are doing something wrong, or that they are doing many things wrong, the constructive reaction should be to evaluate and process the message, not punish the messenger. As the immigrant Emergent rise in income and status, they, too, would move beyond eligibility for any special assistance.

The problems of the Abandoned have to be attacked on every level, all at once. It can't be an either-or proposition— either we set up enterprise zones, with tax breaks, to encourage the formation of small businesses, or we intervene directly with government-sponsored jobs programs. We have to do both.

We have to accelerate the process of tearing down dangerous, decrepit housing projects and replacing them with units that are less Stalinist in scale and easier to make secure. We have to intervene directly with families to break daisy-chain cycles of teen pregnancy; we have to rebuild and re-staff the schools; we have to give young men and women something to dream about beyond the confines of the neighborhoods where they live.

And speaking of neighborhoods, one part of the solution to the all-but-intractable problems of the Abandoned has to be a wholesale embrace of gentrification. Both the Abandoned and their advocates need to see this wrenching process as both desirable and necessary.

From the point of view of the people being displaced, there is a lot not to like about gentrification. It yanks people out of neighborhoods where their families may have had roots for generations. It entices homeowners to sell at prices that are a fraction of what they could demand just a few years later. It completes the shredding of what once were healthy, vibrant communities.

But neighborhoods that become gentrified have, by definition, already disintegrated, which means that the toxic and seemingly inexorable Abandoned pathology has already set in. Research indicates not just that concentrated black poverty is self-sustaining but that the fact of racial segregation may be the most important impediment to turning around a neighborhood's decline. So to the extent that gentrification breaks up tough knots of Abandoned poverty and scatters people to the winds, including to other areas that might be just as poor but are more racially integrated, the process actually can be beneficial to the displaced—with one big caveat.

The caveat is that the displaced cannot simply be forced

215

into another all-black ghetto—one that is more remote, with even fewer amenities and services. This is largely what has happened in Washington and some other cities, and the result is that the problem just gets moved, not solved.

By far the best solution—and, yes, it costs money—is to preserve or create low-income housing that allows the Abandoned to stay in place while the neighborhood gentrifies around them. All this is well-known to municipal officials across the nation; the problem is the expense, both in initial outlay and eventual tax receipts. The bursting of the real estate bubble and the implosion of the subprime mortgage industry have not had many positive effects, but the slowing of the gentrification steamroller and the return of property values to more rational levels should provide some breathing room for effective housing policies. An explicit goal should be ameliorating the racial segregation of Abandoned communities, and one way of doing that is to encourage and manage gentrification in ways that create diverse neighborhoods—ones that include not just affluent white newcomers but also low-income black survivors.

A domestic Marshall Plan aimed at Abandoned black America will be expensive, and politically it will be a hard sell. For reasons that I doubt anyone really understands, it seems to be much easier to convince Americans and their elected officials to spend hundreds of billions of dollars for comprehensive nation-building programs in faraway places like Iraq and Afghanistan than to fund comparable initiatives in their own hometowns. We're willing to pay young men in Kabul to hand over their weapons, to build schools for them so they can learn marketable skills, to create jobs for them so they can stop selling drugs. We decline to do the same for young men in Kansas City. Someday, perhaps, someone will explain why this is supposed to make sense.

A Marshall Plan to attack entrenched African American poverty, dysfunction, and violence should be framed as a cognate of the original Marshall Plan: a costly, but ultimately profitable, investment in America's national security. I doubt that it can be sold to the public and to Congress at all unless it is made explicit that the intent is not to give any special advantages to Mainstream black families that most Americans consider to be middle class or even affluent. Even given the nation's serious burden of deficit and debt, designing and building a bridge to bring the Abandoned into the Mainstream is not beyond our reach. It took just days to come up with nearly a trillion dollars to save the international financial system. The United States spends almost as much on defense as all the other nations of the world combined—an incredible 48 percent of the global total. We can find the money. We just have to find the political will.

* * *

We also have to find the political leadership.

President Obama has taken the position that his initiatives, to the extent that they are aimed at helping the working class and the poor, will inevitably benefit African Americans to a greater degree than most other groups. If black people are less likely to have health insurance, for example, then health-care reform that provides insurance will have a greater impact in black communities; if energy legislation creates thousands of new "green" jobs and black unemployment is nearly twice as high as white unemployment, then African Americans should see disproportionate rewards.

After a grace period of a year or so, some African American activists and intellectuals began to complain that Obama's race-neutral approach was not bold enough to address the crisis in Abandoned black America. Perhaps the most visible and voluble of the critics was commentator Tavis Smiley, who convened a Black Agenda Summit in Chicago, Obama's hometown, to press for more urgent and targeted action. "The bottom line is the president needs to take the issues of black America more seriously because black folks are catching hell, number one," he said. "Number two: This theory that a rising tide lifting all boats—that theory was soundly dismissed. Thirdly, because black people are suffering disproportionately, it requires a disproportionate response."[12] With equal volume and assertiveness, Obama was defended by a leader whom many people would have expected to be on the other side of the issue: the Reverend Al Sharpton. There was no need, Sharpton said, for Obama to "ballyhoo" a specific black agenda. He argued, in effect, that progressive policies could be targeted to focus on inner-city or rural communities without being specifically labeled as instruments of black uplift.

Sharpton had the keener sense of public relations and the political moment. Polls showed that the most vehement critics of the first African American president—a majority of Tea Party protesters, for example—already believed that Obama's programs favored black Americans over others. The reality is that some whites were always going to suspect Obama of favoritism, no matter what he said or did. Being a "first black" anything always involves bending over backward not just to be evenhanded but to demonstrate that evenhandedness.

On substance, though, Smiley has a point. The crisis in Abandoned black America is unique: It is profound, multi-generational, and in some ways worsening. Between 2000 and 2005, the segment of black American households at the bottom, earning less than $15,000 a year, grew from 23.1 percent to 26 percent.[13] Any president could make a compelling argument for focused and sustained attention to the plight of the Abandoned. Sharpton is right that labels don't matter—you could call it an "inner-city agenda" or something like that, and of course you wouldn't make an all-out assault on black poverty and dysfunction so exclusive that it poured government funds into the mean streets of Compton while totally ignoring the barrios of East Los Angeles. Whatever the label, though, a Marshall Plan for inner-city America is going to involve a lot of resources being directed toward a lot of black people—and for the first black president, there would inevitably be political blowback.

But Obama has an important card that he can play: means testing of affirmative action programs. He can declare that from now on, the black Mainstream should be on its own—in exchange for the political leeway to concentrate money and attention on the Abandoned.

He would need support, however, from other black leaders and opinion-makers—from members of the Congressional Black Caucus, for example, as well as big-city mayors, the major civil rights organizations, and other important actors. For African American officeholders, this would require considerable courage. The district of Congressman James Clyburn, for example, includes areas with some of the worst rural and urban poverty in South Carolina. But he also represents Mainstream communities whose residents are more likely to vote and who are in a better position to give campaign contributions than his Abandoned constituents.

A new generation of black political leadership at the municipal level is already trying variations of the Marshall Plan approach. When Newark mayor Cory Booker—a Stanford University and Yale Law School graduate, as well as a Rhodes scholar—first ran for the city's top job in 2002, he was derided as "not black enough" by longtime incumbent Sharpe James. Booker lost that race, but ran again in 2006 and won. Booker has made a point of living in the city's Abandoned neighborhoods throughout his public career: While he was campaigning in 2006, he was one of the last remaining tenants in Brick Towers, a crime-ridden, drug-infested housing project that since has been torn down. On taking office, Booker made safe streets a top priority, overhauling the police department, installing a system of surveillance cameras, and sometimes going out on late-night patrols himself. Between 2006 and 2008, murders in Newark fell by 36 percent, shootings by 41 percent, rapes by 30 percent, and car thefts by 26 percent, according to a glowing 2009 profile in *Time* magazine. In March 2010, Newark had its first murder-free month in forty-four years.

Booker doubled the amount of affordable housing under development, slashed the city's budget deficit in half, attracted more than $100 million in private philanthropic funding to support school reform and other initiatives, and cut his own salary twice. He turned down an offer from President Obama to be the new administration's urban policy czar, deciding instead to continue the work he had begun in Newark. That work is still far from done—more than 28 percent of Newark's residents live below the poverty line. But in a city whose population has been declining since 1960—at times gradually, at times precipitously—the 2010 census was expected to show a slight increase.

In Washington, Mayor Adrian Fenty staked his political future on an all-out attempt to repair and reform the broken public school system. His abrasive schools chancellor, Michelle Rhee, steamrolled the powerful teachers' union and won permission, basically, to reshape the schools however she wanted. But the teaching profession is a Mainstream sacred cow; there was a time, not long ago, when education was one of the few career options available to African Americans who today would likely become investment bankers, lobbyists, or architects. Some of the political damage that Fenty suffered was self-inflicted, but the upshot is that he achieved a modest gain for the Abandoned while losing much of his Mainstream support.

Maybe that's the way it has to be, however. Maybe some politicians are going to have to fall on their swords. The one unacceptable course of action is to do nothing, to try nothing new, to tolerate the intolerable status quo—and doom the Abandoned to fall even further behind.

10 · WE KNOW WHO WE ARE. BUT WHO WILL WE BE?

Now that disintegration has cleaved one black America into four, will we still nod to each other when we pass on the street?

It has been the custom for as long as I can remember: When a black person is walking down the sidewalk, particularly in a mostly white environment—the business district of a city like Denver, say, or a trendy shopping strip in Santa Monica—and meets another black person walking in the opposite direction, it is natural for these strangers to acknowledge each other with a small gesture or a mumbled greeting as they pass. We don't go out of our way for these encounters, and there's certainly nothing obligatory about them. Often they barely even register, although I'd guess I may have as many as a dozen in the course of a day. Usually, at least for me, all that's involved is the making of eye contact followed by a quick nod of the head. The whole thing isn't much more than a reflex, but it feels satisfying. If I had to explain, I'd say it was an affirmation of something shared, something remembered, something understood, something cherished. It is an acknowledgment that even as total strangers, what we have in common is our racial identity.

But I have to wonder if that is still true. I have to ask whether black Americans, divided as they are by the process of disintegration, still have enough shared experiences, values, hopes, fears, and dreams that they define and claim a single racial identity—and feel a racial solidarity powerful enough to connect, if only for an instant, strangers who may never see each other again.

I give the little nod without even thinking about it. Is it my imagination, or are fewer people nodding back?

* * *

We now know that in terms of biology, race means nothing. This has long been intuitively obvious, at least to non-racists, but now we have proof. The deciphering of the genetic code shows that external features such as skin color and hair texture indicate nothing about a person's nature, intelligence, or capabilities, and that it would make just as much sense to group people by any other arbitrarily chosen markers—blood type, say, or ability to whistle.

Human beings are one species, and what we call race is really just a crude marker for proximity. People who live near one another tend to share genetic material, and this tendency was much more pronounced throughout the eons of human evolution when groups were settled and the only means of transportation was walking. Thus it follows that people whose ancestors lived closer together are more likely to share genetic traits—skin color, for example—than people whose ancestors lived far apart. Notions of there being precisely three major "races" of people whom we classify as white, black, and yellow—or perhaps five with the addition of red people and brown people—are eighteenth-century rationalizations for the brutal use of European technology in the colonial subjugation of populations that lacked firearms, sailing ships, and horses. People who lived a thousand years ago would have thought this classification system absurd; people who live a thousand years from now will surely think it barbaric.

But we also know that whatever characteristics we use to define and assign "race" tell us even less about black people than about other "races." Because Africa is the landmass where *Homo sapiens* evolved, and where humans remained for most of our existence, Africans (and the diaspora, including African Americans) display an extraordinarily wide range of genetic diversity. Of all the DNA mutations that found their way into the human genome over the eons that our distant ancestors spent confined to the mother continent, only some were carried to other parts of the globe by the small groups of wanderers who left Africa and eventually populated Asia, Europe, Australia, and the Americas. As a result, two individuals who are both considered black might easily be more dissimilar to each other, at the genetic level, than either is to a person who belongs to another "race." Imagine an African American couple on their first date, dining at a restaurant called Luigi's. Either or both of them might have more in common with the Italian American waiter who brings them their pasta, as measured by common DNA sequences, than they do with each other.[1]

Race is a human invention, a social construct, and its parameters shift over time. Racial identity has always been fluid, based not on objective reality but on perception and self-image. Europeans once held the notion that the Irish were a separate "race" with distinctive characteristics, as were the Germans, the Slavs, and of course the oft-persecuted Jews; now we think of all these peoples as "white." The San people of South Africa have a different genetic and cultural history from that of the Bantu people of the Congo, but both are now considered "black." There is no valid way to divide people into racial categories—which means that the important thing, where race is concerned, is how people are seen and how they see themselves.

Some of the most interesting recent data about African Americans' self-image comes from that stunning 2007 survey by the Pew Research Center, in which 37 percent of black Americans said that black people in this country could no longer "be thought of as a single race." There was no follow-up question to explore just what those people—an incredible four out of ten—had in mind when they made that judgment. But there are powerful suggestions that the separation perceived by so many African Americans is both economic and cultural.

The Pew survey asked African American respondents which of two statements was closer to their own views: "Racial discrimination is the main reason why many black people can't get ahead these days," or "Blacks who can't get ahead in this country are mostly responsible for their own condition." When the question was asked in 1994, a majority—56 percent—blamed discrimination; only 34 percent held the black poor responsible for their failure to "get ahead." But in the 2007 survey, those attitudes were reversed: A full 53 percent of African American respondents blamed poor black people for their plight, while just 30 percent said that racial discrimination was making it impossible for poor African Americans to better themselves. This says nothing about racial identity, but perhaps it does tell us something about racial solidarity.

Another set of questions inquired about values. Asked whether "the values held by middle-class black people and the values held by poor black people" had become more similar or more different in the past decade, 61 percent said values had diverged; 31 percent said the values of poor and middle-class African Americans now have "only a little" or "almost nothing" in common.[2]

To put it in the terms of this book, it seems that most African Americans now blame the Abandoned for their own poverty and dysfunction. Most black Americans see a widening gap between the values held by the Mainstream and the Abandoned. And almost a third of African Americans describe the chasm as so wide that it is hard to imagine how it could be bridged.

* * *

Solidarity has been one of black Americans' most powerful weapons in the struggle for freedom, justice, and opportunity. There was often sharp disagreement about how to get from where we were to where we needed to go—the argument between Booker T. Washington and W. E. B. DuBois, for example, or the many differences in approach among such titans of the civil rights movement as Roy Wilkins of the NAACP, Whitney Young of the National Urban League, and Martin Luther King. I once interviewed Julian Bond about his time with the Student Nonviolent Coordinating Committee, and I asked which was the most passionate argument he could recall from those heady days. He thought for a moment, then a moment longer. "Wow, there were so many," he said.

Finally he settled on a two-day, yelling-and-screaming row over whether the SNCC would participate in the first Selma-to-Montgomery march on March 7, 1965. Most SNCC leaders believed the march would be a distraction from the group's primary mission: grassroots organizing. Some even thought it was a made-for-television stunt, with clear potential for violence that could get out of hand. Others believed that at a moment so fraught with both peril and potential, an organization like the SNCC simply could not remain on the sidelines. The executive committee eventually voted not to join the march officially, but to tell members they could participate as individuals if they chose. The marchers were met by state-sponsored mob violence at the Edmund Pettus Bridge, a bloody confrontation that is remembered as one of the most galvanizing moments of the whole civil rights era. Ironically, an SNCC leader, Congressman John Lewis, was one of the day's great heroes.

Yet despite clashes over methods back then, there was no real dispute about what the agenda for black Americans should include: the right to vote, the right to a better education, the right to use public accommodations, the right to live beyond the confines of assigned ghettos, the right to live without fear of oppression by police, the right to live without fear of violent attack by hooded, cross-burning terrorists. Those were the short-term goals. Longer term, there was political empowerment, economic development, and full incorporation of African Americans into the worlds of business, academia, the media, and so forth. It was clear where black Americans needed to go, and there was not really much of an argument about the kinds of policies we should advocate and support.

Crudely put, what was good for poor people was good for black people, since so many black people were poor. Conversely, what was good for rich people was bad for black people, since so few black people were rich. The economic theories of John Maynard Keynes were good for black people because expensive government programs were necessary for the project of uplift; if deficit spending led to inflation, that was no great disaster because black people had so little capital to protect. The economic theories of Milton Friedman, which saw inflation as a scourge and advocated tight control over the money supply, were bad for black people. In the larger sense, it was generally true that what was good for the established order was bad for black people, who didn't belong to the Establishment; and what was upsetting to the established order was good for black people because it created new opportunities for outsiders like us.

That was then.

Today, black Americans' fundamental rights are secure. To be sure, these rights are not always and universally observed. A year into the administration of the first African American president, federal authorities accused a Mississippi school district of deliberately enforcing a policy of segregation by transferring students to designated schools according to race. Postmortems on the subprime mortgage crisis unearthed evidence that worrisome numbers of black home buyers were steered by agents and brokers into riskier loans, at higher interest rates, than whites with similar incomes and credit ratings. African Americans are tremendously overrepresented in the prison population nationwide, and much of the disparity would be eliminated if the law did not treat crack cocaine, which is mostly bought and sold in Abandoned black communities, so much more harshly than it treats the identical drug in powder form, which is the way whites tend to buy and sell it. When presented with obvious examples of unequal treatment such as these, it is easy for the four black Americas to agree: Here is an injustice, here is how to fix it.

There also is no real dispute about issues that involve symbolism. When a white entertainer utters a phrase like "nappy-headed ho's" or uses the word "nigger," all four black Americas concur in outrage. It would be wrong to trivialize these kinds of incidents; symbolic is not a synonym for insignificant. Dignity and respect matter. And given the arc of African American history, they matter a lot.

But far more important than symbols are the big, concrete, urgent concerns that some black Americans now face—issues on which consensus has been elusive and momentum has stalled.

Earlier in these pages, I proposed that our most urgent priority should be an all-out assault on the stubborn, self-perpetuating poverty and dysfunction of the Abandoned, channeling into this effort the affirmative action preferences and resources that currently go mostly to the Mainstream. I am confident that many in the Mainstream would support such an effort—philosophically, at least.

But African Americans who have only recently managed to attain middle-class status would complain, understandably, that they need all the support they can get just to keep from falling back. And even some in what might be called the upper Mainstream—professionals with six-figure incomes— find themselves handcuffed by the ten-to-one wealth ratio between whites and blacks. An illustration: Acquaintances of mine, a couple about my age, wanted a better education for their two children than the District of Columbia public schools could offer. So they sent them to an excellent private school where tuition has climbed to nearly $30,000 a year. The couple makes a combined $230,000 a year, which is a lot. But like most successful African Americans (and many other Americans, of course, regardless of race), they built their whole lives essentially from scratch. There was no trust fund to help pay for the children's schooling, no fat and timely checks from grandma and grandpa. The couple ended up draining the equity in their house to pay those education costs and maintain a comfortable lifestyle. When their son got accepted by an expensive private college, they were already tapped out. For parents in that situation, it would be easy to believe, on an intellectual level, that affirmative action scholarships should go to those with the most critical need, the Abandoned. Yet it would be hard not to accept one of those scholarships if it were offered.

The economic interests of the Mainstream and those of the Abandoned coincide in the long run; ultimately, the goal is for the Abandoned to become Mainstream. But those interests diverge along the way. Two obvious goals for African Americans are consolidating decades of impressive gains into solid, multigenerational wealth; and doing whatever it takes to uplift the millions still trapped in desperate, multigenerational poverty. One project benefits the Mainstream; the other benefits the Abandoned. There is no obvious reason for universal agreement on which should have first claim on finite government resources and attention.

This is a moment when the Transcendent are in an unprecedented position to lead. I refer not just to political leaders like

President Obama and House majority whip James Clyburn but also to the black men and women who have risen to great power in business, entertainment, communications, and other fields. They have more authority than earlier generations could have imagined, greater resources at their disposal than ever before, and powerful influence not just among African Americans but throughout the larger society. Polls show that traditional leadership groups like the NAACP and the National Urban League have lost much, if not most, of their standing among black Americans; these venerable institutions are still respected, but it is safe to say that no one hangs on every word uttered by Benjamin Jealous or Marc Morial, who are their current leaders. Both men are smart, creative, and dynamic, but neither they nor their successors will ever be able to speak to and for black America the way that Roy Wilkins and Whitney Young once did. Today's Transcendent black Americans have far more clout as individuals—when Oprah Winfrey says jump, legions ask how high—but there are no leaders who can claim to represent all four black Americas.

What the Transcendents can do, at a minimum, is make a difference in their own areas of power and influence. To take one example, I made clear earlier that I didn't care for the movie *Precious*. But by giving it their backing, Oprah Winfrey and Tyler Perry provided a platform for a host of talented African Americans who otherwise might never have been noticed. Lee Daniels now joins the select group of Hollywood directors who can have their choice of projects. Geoffrey Fletcher, who won an Oscar for the screenplay, now will have his scripts read with interest rather than tossed into some pile. The stories that these artists go on to tell may provoke, uplift, inspire—or they may not. But at least they will be told.

In a similar manner, Transcendent CEOs can't rescue the Abandoned, but they can serve as localized engines of economic development for the Mainstream by making certain that their companies actually practice diversity rather than just preach it. If they ensure that qualified and capable African Americans are represented among their executive teams, suppliers, and outside bankers, lawyers, and accountants, they will leave behind a far greater legacy than whatever the final numbers say on the balance sheet.

There is Barack Obama, of course, who technically does represent all four black Americas—and belongs to two of them, as a Transcendent and a double Emergent. But Obama represents the whole color wheel of America—white, brown, yellow, indeterminate, whatever. It is inconceivable that the president of the United States could see himself, or have others see him, as a "black leader."

It's time, in any event, to retire the term "black leader" for good. At this point in our progress, it sounds patronizing. Given the achievements of African Americans over the past four decades, we are hardly a bunch of followers who need to be told what to think and do. More important, leadership implies coordinated movement in a specified direction. It implies an agenda, and African Americans don't have one. We have many. At times they overlap, and at times they conflict.

Politically it is likely that all four black Americas will remain loyal to the Democratic Party for the foreseeable future—not only because of Obama, whom African Americans are unlikely to desert, but because the modern Republican Party has made so little effort to attract black voters, or even to stop doing their best to drive them away. (Naming Michael Steele as the first African American chairman of the party doesn't count, its tokenism was so apparent.) In 2009, the Transcendent businesswoman Sheila Johnson, a Democrat, made headlines when she publicly supported Republican Bob McDonnell for governor of Virginia—but she was embarrassed when he promptly declared Confederate History Month with a proclamation that neglected to mention the tiny little detail known as slavery. This strikes me as typical. I have always believed that it would be good if Republicans made a genuine attempt to win African American votes—which would make Democrats have to work harder to keep them—but the reality is that this doesn't seem likely anytime soon.

So the Democrats are the only game in town, and not since the presidential campaigns of Jesse Jackson and Al Sharpton have the party's Transcendent bigwigs or its Mainstream rank and file challenged the party's leadership from an explicitly black perspective. Rather, African Americans have won genuine power in the party by working within the system. For instance, Congressman Clyburn, the second-most-powerful African American in Washington after Obama, was instrumental in finally getting the president's health-care-reform legislation passed. As the third-ranking member of the House of Representatives, he also has managed to keep a stream of much-needed funds flowing to cash-strapped historically black colleges and universities. Clyburn is a graduate of South Carolina State University, which is just down the street from the house where I grew up. African Americans should continue to use their power and influence within the Democratic Party, and maybe someday the Republicans will come calling with a bouquet of flowers.

Meanwhile, it's all but inevitable that at times the four black Americas will rub up against one another, and the points of contact may chafe. There is already friction between the immigrant Emergent and the Abandoned, who complain of being exploited by immigrant-black-owned businesses just as they once complained about neighborhood stores whose proprietors were white, Jewish, or Korean. The Mainstream have long whispered their disapproval of how Emergent immigrants were taking—or, to be honest, winning—college admissions slots that some believe should go to the native-born. Now, increasingly, those objections are being spoken out loud.

The biracial Emergent have the advantage of straddling two worlds—but also the disadvantage of being able to reject neither. Those who embrace African American identity with no reservation, as President Obama did, are in turn embraced warmly by the other black Americas. Those who have more difficulty composing a coherent racial self are viewed with a certain cool ambiguity.

One example of this involves Washington mayor Adrian Fenty, who is biracial and was elected in a landslide, winning every precinct in the city. Once in office, he put fewer African Americans in key, high-profile posts than his predecessor black mayors had done; his cool, technocratic style had none of the glad-handing, back-slapping empathy that voters were used to from the likes of Marion Barry, who emerged as one of Fenty's harshest critics. An impression was somehow created that the mayor was acting with favoritism toward white residents—or, I think more accurately, that he was acting without favoritism toward black residents. As he prepared to stand for reelection in 2010, he had a campaign war chest that looked big enough to overwhelm any challenger. But his poll numbers among African Americans—in both Mainstream and Abandoned neighborhoods—were plummeting, and I believe it is fair to say that the reason had to do less with any of his specific words or deeds than with unease about his sense of identity.

The Abandoned increasingly stand apart and alone. They resent immigrant Emergents who use their communities as stepping-stones, Mainstream do-gooders who come to lecture them by day but make sure to leave before nightfall, and Transcendents who talk black but in every sense act white. The rest of us moved away and left them to their own devices, without the tools or the knowledge to better themselves. They noticed.

W. E. B. DuBois famously wrote that "the problem of the Twentieth Century is the color-line." I believe the problem of the twenty-first century is the problem of the Abandoned. The longer we wait to solve it, the harder it will be to even know where to begin.

And the longer we wait, the longer we forestall the possibility of a day when race ceases to be the defining attribute of African Americans. Throughout our history, other groups of outsiders, such as the Irish, the Italians, and the Jews, have been looked down upon, stigmatized, and discriminated against, but eventually through hard work and sacrifice have won their rightful place in American society. African Americans have overcome far greater obstacles to accomplish the same feat—and yet race still separates us, preoccupies us, and defines us.

There is no longer one black America, no longer a complete sense of racial solidarity based on clearly defined common interests. But there remains one black racial identity that the majority of African Americans—Mainstream, Abandoned, Transcendent, and Emergent—still share. As long as the Abandoned remain buried in both society's and their own dysfunction, with diminishing hope of ever being able to escape, the rest of us cannot feel that we have truly escaped, either. We cannot begin to un-hyphenate ourselves. Certainly, DuBois's "color-line" has been shifted to entrap fewer black Americans, but at the same time it has become more impregnable. The challenge for every American now is to erase it once and for all.

NOTES

1: "Black America" Doesn't Live Here Anymore

1. Carmen DeNavas-Walt, Bernadette D. Proctor, and Cheryl Hill Lee, *Income, Poverty, and Health Insurance Coverage in the United States: 2005* (Washington, D.C.: U.S. Census Bureau, 2006), 34.
2. Ibid.
3. Ibid., 31.
4. Mary Mederios Kent, "Immigration and America's Black Population," *Population Bulletin* 62, 4 (2007): 4.
5. Sara Rimer and Karen W. Arenson, "Top Colleges Take More Blacks, But Which Ones?," *The New York Times*, June 24, 2004.
6. David R. Harris and Hiromi Ono, "Cohabitation, Marriage, and Markets: A New Look at Intimate Interracial Relationships," in *Discussion Paper* (Ann Arbor, MI: Institute for Social Research, University of Michigan, 2003).
7. "Optimism About Black Progress Declines: Blacks See Growing Values Gap Between Poor and Middle Class," Pew Research Center, November 13, 2007.
8. D.C. Public Schools website, available at http://dcatlas.dcgis .dc.gov/schoolprofile/.
9. Eugene Robinson, "Which Black America?," *The Washington Post*, October 9, 2007.
10. Charles Johnson, "The End of the Black American Narrative," *The American Scholar* (Summer 2008): 6; also available at www.the americanscholar.org/the-end-of-the-black-american-narrative/.

2: When We Were One

1. Booker T. Washington, "Atlanta Compromise Speech," September 18, 1985, Booker T. Washington Collection, African American Odyssey, American Memory (Washington, D.C.: Library of Congress).
2. W. E. B. DuBois, "Of Mr. Booker T. Washington and Others," in *The Souls of Black Folk* (Chicago: A. C. McClurg & Company, 1903), 33.
3. Ray Stannard Baker, *Following the Color Line: An Account of Negro Citizenship in the American Democracy* (New York: Doubleday, Page & Company, 1908), 9–10.
4. Ibid., 9.
5. W. E. B. DuBois, "A Litany of Atlanta," in *The Book of American Negro Poetry* (New York: Harcourt, Brace and Company, 1922), 49–54.
6. Baker, 14.
7. Ibid., 16–17.
8. Stewart E. Tolnay, "The African American 'Great Migration' and Beyond," *Annual Review of Sociology* 29 (2003): 209–32.
9. "Optimism About Black Progress Declines: Blacks See Growing Values Gap Between Poor and Middle Class," Pew Research Center, November 13, 2007.

3: Parting of the Ways

1. Sam Smith, "A Short History of Black Washington," *The Progressive Review* (2003).
2. Ben W. Gilbert et al., *Ten Blocks from the White House: Anatomy of the Washington Riots of 1968* (New York: F. A. Praeger, 1968), 23–24.
3. Chicago Center for Working Class Studies, Community Walk Project www.workingclassstudies.org; www.labortrail.org; www.community walk.com.
4. Thomas J. Sugrue, "Motor City: The Story of Detroit," *History Now* 11 (March 2007); also available at www.gilderlehrman.org/history now/03_2007/historian6.php.
5. U.S. Department of Housing and Urban Development website, available at www.hud.gov/offices/fheo/FHLaws/index.cfm.
6. "Report of the National Advisory Commission on Civil Disorders," available at www.eisenhowerfoundation.org/docs/kerner.pdf, 1.
7. *Loving v. Virginia*, U.S. Supreme Court, available at www.law .cornell.edu/supct/html/historics/USSC_CR_0388_0001_ZO .html, 2.

8. Ibid.
9. Esteban J. Parra et al., "Estimating African American Admixture Proportions by Use of Population-Specific Alleles," *The American Journal of Human Genetics* 63, 6 (December 1998): 1839–51.
10. U.S. Census Bureau, "Population by Race and Hispanic or Latino Origin for the United States: 1990 and 2000 (PHC-T-1)," Table 2, available at www.census.gov/population/www/cen2000/briefs/phc-t1/index.html.
11. Mary Mederios Kent, "Immigration and America's Black Population," *Population Bulletin* 62, 4 (2007): 13.
12. Ibid., 6.
13. Carmen DeNavas-Walt, Bernadette D. Proctor, and Cheryl Hill Lee, *Income, Poverty, and Health Insurance Coverage in the United States: 2005* (Washington, D.C.: U.S. Census Bureau, 2006), 31.

4: The Mainstream: A Double Life

1. All figures from U.S. Census Bureau, available at http://quickfacts.census.gov/qfd/index.html.
2. Ibid.
3. St. Clair Drake and Horace Cayton, *Black Metropolis: A Study of Negro Life in a Northern City* (New York: Harcourt, Brace and Company, 1945), 226–27.
4. Ibid., 239–42.
5. Carmen DeNavas-Walt, Bernadette D. Proctor, and Cheryl Hill Lee, *Income, Poverty, and Health Insurance Coverage in the United States: 2005* (Washington, D.C.: U.S. Census Bureau, 2006), 32–34.
6. Ibid., 34.
7. U.S. Census Bureau, "Current Population Survey," Historical Tables, Table A-2, available at www.census.gov/population/www/socdemo/educ-attn.html.
8. Jeffrey M. Humphreys, *The Multicultural Economy 2008* (Athens, GA: Selig Center for Economic Growth, University of Georgia, 2008), 14; see Table 1.
9. Media Matters for America, September 21, 2007, available at mediamatters.org/research/200709210007.
10. U.S. Census Bureau, "U.S. Population Projections, Released 2008 (Based on Census 2000)," Summary Table 2, available at www.census.gov/population/www/projections/summarytables.html.

11. Stephen Provasnik, Linda L. Shafer, and Thomas D. Snyder, *Historically Black Colleges and Universities, 1976 to 2001* (Washington, D.C.: U.S. Department of Education), 4.

5: The Abandoned: No Way Out

1. Greater New Orleans Community Data Center, see Pre-Katrina Poverty Map, available at www.gnocdc.org.
2. Bruce Katz, "Concentrated Poverty in New Orleans and Other American Cities," *The Chronicle of Higher Education* (August 4, 2006); also available at www.brookings.edu/opinions/2006/0804cities _katz.aspx.
3. Greater New Orleans Community Data Center.
4. The following summary is taken from *A Failure of Initiative: Final Report of the Select Bipartisan Committee to Investigate the Preparation for and Response to Hurricane Katrina*, Congressional Reports: H. Rpt. 109–377 (Washington, D.C.: Government Publishing Office, 2008), 7–9; available at www.gpoaccess.gov/serialset/ creports/katrina.html.
5. Greater New Orleans Community Data Center.
6. William Julius Wilson, "When Work Disappears: New Implications for Race and Urban Poverty in the Global Economy," Centre for Analysys of Social Exclusion, London School of Economics, November 1998, available at sticerd.lse.ac.uk/dps/case/cp/ paper17.pdf.
7. Greater New Orleans Community Data Center.
8. Ibid.
9. Douglas S. Massey, "American Apartheid: Segregation and the Making of the Underclass," *American Journal of Sociology* 96, 2 (September 1990): 329–57.
10. U.S. Census Bureau, "The 2010 Stastical Abstract: The National Data Book," Table 295: Crimes and Crime Rates by Type of Offense, available at www.census.gov/compendia/statab/cats/ law_enforcement_courts_prisons/crimes_and_crime_rates.html.
11. U.S. Census Bureau, State and County QuickFacts, available at http://quickfacts.census.gov/qfd/states/11000.html.
12. Rose M. Kreider, *Living Arrangements of Children: 2004* (Washington, D.C.: U.S. Census Bureau, February 2008), 4; also available at www.census.gov/prod/2008pubs/p70–114.pdf.

13. William J. Sabol, Heather C. West, and Matthew Cooper, *Prisoners in 2008* (Washington, D.C.: U.S. Bureau of Justice Statistics, 2009), 2; also available at http://bjs.ojp.usdoj.gov/index .cfm?ty=pbdetail&iid=1763.
14. Reuters news story, available at www.reuters.com/article/idUS TRE5AP1EV20091126.

6: The Transcendent: Where None Have Gone Before
1. Shailagh Murray, "Obama Camp Pushes Back on 'Rookie' Ad," *The Washington Post*, January 18, 2008.
2. Katharine Q. Seelye, "BET Founder Slams Obama in South Carolina," *The New York Times*, January 13, 2008.
3. Fox News, December 10, 2007, available at www.foxnews.com/ story/0,2933,316366,00.html.
4. These statistics are available at http://health.usnews.com/health -news/family-health/childrens-health/articles/2010/03/01/risk -of-childhood-obesity-higher-among-minorities.html.
5. Carmen DeNavas-Walt, Bernadette D. Proctor, and Cheryl Hill Lee, *Income, Poverty, and Health Insurance Coverage in the United States: 2005* (Washington, D.C.: U.S. Census Bureau, 2006), 24.
6. *Fox and Friends*, transcript, February 22, 2008.
7. Eugene Robinson, "Black America's New Reality," *The Washington Post*, July 19, 2009.
8. Harold Ford Jr. official website, available at haroldfordjr.com.
9. Michael Barbaro, "Senate Hopeful in New State Airs Evolving Views," *The New York Times*, January 12, 2010.

7: The Emergent (Part 1): Coming to America
1. Mary Mederios Kent, "Immigration and America's Black Population," *Population Bulletin* 62, 4 (2007): 12–14.
2. District of Columbia registry of business names and owners, available at http://app.dctaxi.dc.gov/taxilist.asp.
3. Pamela R. Bennett and Amy Lutz, "How African American Is the Net Black Advantage? Differences in College Attendance Among Immigrant Blacks, Native Blacks, and Whites," *Sociology of Education* 82 (January 2009): 70–100.
4. Kay Deaux et al., "Becoming American: Stereotype Threat Effects

in Afro-Caribbean Immigrant Groups," *Social Psychology Quarterly* 70, 4 (2007): 384–404.

5. Estimate per the Ethiopian Community Center, Washington, D.C.; author interview with a representative from the center.

6. Historical narrative from research by the author for *Coal to Cream* (New York: The Free Press, 1999) and *Last Dance in Havana* (New York: The Free Press, 2004).

8: The Emergent (Part 2): How Black Is Black?

1. Michael J. Rosenfeld and Byung-Soo Kim, "The Independence of Young Adults and the Rise of Interracial and Same-Sex Unions," *American Sociological Review* 70 (2005): 1.

2. Jeffrey S. Passel, Wendy Wang, and Paul Taylor, "Marrying Out," Pew Research Center, available at http://pewresearch.org/pubs/1616/american-marriage-interracial-interethnic?src=prc-latest& proj=peoplepress.

3. Entire text of speech available at my.barackobama.com/page/content/hisownwords.

9: Urgency, Focus, and Sacrifice

1. National Urban League, *The State of Black America 2010: Jobs: Responding to the Crisis* (New York: National Urban League, 2010), 1.

2. U.S. Census Bureau, "U.S. Population Projections, Released 2008 (Based on Census 2000)," Summary Table 2, available at www.census.gov/population/www/projections/summarytables.html.

3. Shamara Riley, "Three Ways to Fix the 'State of Black America,' " thegrio.com, March 26, 2010, available at www.thegrio.com/specials/state-of-black-america/where-the-state-of-black-america-report-goes-wrong.php.

4. Magazine Publishers of America, "African-American/Black Market Profile," New York, 2008, available at www.magazine.org/ASSETS/2457647D5D0A45F7B1735B8ABCFA3C26/market_profile_black.pdf.

5. The account of this incident is drawn from *Washington Post* reports over the course of several weeks, and reflects the best available description of the events and their motivation; see Eugene

Robinson, "The Invisible Underlcass," *The Washington Post*, April 6, 2010.

6. Elijah Anderson, "The Social Ecology of Youth Violence," *Crime and Justice* 24 (1998).

7. Ibid.

8. Ibid.

9. Elijah Anderson, *Code of the Street* (New York: W. W. Norton & Company, Inc., 1999), 26–27.

10. Anderson, "The Social Ecology of Youth Violence."

11. Sam Sanders, "Black Teenage Males Crushed by Unemployment," National Public Radio, January 10, 2010, available at www.npr.org/templates/story/story.php?storyId=122367407.

12. Smiley's comments available at http://voices.washingtonpost.com/44/2010/03/from-tavis-smiley-love-and-cri.html.

13. Carmen DeNavas-Walt, Bernadette D. Proctor, and Cheryl Hill Lee, *Income, Poverty, and Health Insurance Coverage in the United States: 2005* (Washington, D.C.: U.S. Census Bureau, 2006), 34.

10: We Know Who We Are. But Who Will We Be?

1. Esteban J. Parra et al., "Estimating African American Admixture Proportions by Use of Population-Specific Alleles," *The American Journal of Human Genetics* 63, 6 (December 1998): 1839–51.

2. "Optimism About Black Progress Declines: Blacks See Growing Values Gap Between Poor and Middle Class," Pew Research Center, November 13, 2007.

INDEX

ABOUT THE AUTHOR

EUGENE ROBINSON joined *The Washington Post* in 1980 and has served as London bureau chief, foreign editor, and, currently, associate editor and columnist. Robinson, who has been a Nieman Fellow at Harvard, was awarded the Pulitzer Prize for distinguished commentary in 2009. He appears frequently on MSNBC as a political analyst. *Disintegration* is his third book.